Penguin

YOU CAN DO IT!

Paul Hanna is regarded as one of Australia's leading motivational speakers. He is living proof that if you set your goals and follow them with tenacity and perseverance, you can achieve big things. From humble beginnings he has risen rapidly to become in constant demand as a consultant to blue-chip corporations like McDonald's, Qantas, BMW and Optus.

When he left school at the age of sixteen, Paul, like many young Australians, did not have a clear idea of what he wanted to do. However, on his first overseas trip he fell in love with travel. To maintain this passion he joined the travel industry and worked his way up to Product Manager at Qantas Airways, where he designed and developed holidays for Australians.

In 1988, after a successful career that included working with some of the heavyweights in the hospitality industry, Paul left Qantas Airways to start a management consultancy. More than a decade on, his client list reads like a who's who of Australia's corporate elite. His other books are *The Mini Motivator, Believe and Achieve!* and *The Money Motivator.*

Paul lives in Sydney.

'Paul Hanna inspires our young managers. He instils in them a desire to do their best and to excel in their private and professional lives. As a result, there is a direct benefit for both the individuals and the business. We have already sent over 3000 people to Paul Hanna's seminars and will provide many more with the same opportunity.'

Charlie Bell
Managing Director/CEO, McDonald's Australia Ltd

'Wow, what a speaker. Our people scored Paul Hanna 5 out of 5 and are still speaking about his presentation nearly a year later. His seminars with our people and their partners are enlightening and gave us a clearer and more positive understanding of our partner's position, which we may not have recognised in the past.'

Peter Capp
Head of Financial Planning, Colonial Financial Planning

'Paul's talks are like a Lolly Gobble Bliss Bomb for the mind. He uses simple but telling analogies that suddenly explode to make you think about yourself and your personal goals. The overall effect is refreshing, challenging, invigorating but satisfying. Long live the storyteller.'

Dick Simpson
Director, Residential, Optus Communications

'Paul's sessions have become synonymous with the word "success" at Westpac. A large number of our staff have attended his workshops and besides improvements in personal lives, the results at work, especially in the area of increased sales, have been spectacular. The simple techniques and powerful messages, delivered by an accomplished speaker, have taught many of our people how to take control of their destiny and enjoy the journey of life. "Attitude determines altitude" has become a catch-cry within our organisation.'

Ken Wright
General Manager, Investments & Insurance, Westpac Banking Corporation

'The feedback from all of our people has been absolutely sensational! Indeed this has been the audience response each time we have used Paul's presentation around Australia.'

Bernie Smith
Toyota Australia

'Yes, the title of this book says it all. Paul has shown so many people how to refocus their attitudes to "life". Now there is a permanent reference manual – to use before and after hearing him present!'

Howard Davy
Broker & Multi Agency Manager, National Mutual

'Paul Hanna's ability is unique. He makes you quickly realise that if you want to achieve success, only you can make it happen. No excuses. Paul shows people how to knock down the barriers to success, and pre-set their own level of success and go for it.'

Robin Honeychurch
Zone Manager, SA/NT, AMP

'I have seen many speakers and would rate Paul Hanna's approach and presentation as the best I have seen.'

Steve Lotter
General Manager, Sales, Toyota Australia

'The response from our people has been extremely positive and I have thoroughly enjoyed the experience of working with a true professional.'

David Kaylor
BMW Australia

Also by Paul Hanna

The Mini Motivator
Believe and Achieve!
The Money Motivator

YOU CAN DO IT!

PAUL HANNA

PENGUIN BOOKS

The publisher would be pleased to hear from the copyright owner of any of the poems reproduced in *You Can Do It!*, as despite extensive research, we are unable to confirm authorship of them.

Penguin Books Australia Ltd
487 Maroondah Highway, PO Box 257
Ringwood, Victoria 3134, Australia
Penguin Books Ltd
Harmondsworth, Middlesex, England
Penguin Putnam Inc.
375 Hudson Street, New York, New York 10014, USA
Penguin Books Canada Limited
10 Alcorn Avenue, Toronto, Ontario, Canada M4V 3B2
Penguin Books (NZ) Ltd
Cnr Rosedale and Airborne Roads, Albany, Auckland, New Zealand
Penguin Books (South Africa) (Pty) Ltd
5 Watkins Street, Denver Ext 4, 2094, South Africa
Penguin Books India (P) Ltd
11, Community Centre, Panchsheel Park, New Delhi 110 017, India

First published by Penguin Books Australia Ltd 1997

18 17 16 15

Typeset in 10/14½ pt Optima by Midland Typesetters, Maryborough, Victoria
Printed in Australia by Australian Print Group, Maryborough, Victoria

National Library of Australia
Cataloguing-in-Publication data:

Hanna, Paul, 1960– .
  You can do it!

  ISBN 0 14 026069 2.

  1. Success. I. Title.

158

www.penguin.com.au

To each and every person
who has been to one of my presentations

Thank you

To be a success,

BE FIRST

BE DARING

BE DIFFERENT

Ray Kroc
Founder, at age 52,
of McDonald's Restaurants

CONTENTS

Introduction

10.20 am, 7 January 1975
Cameron Wing Heart Transplant Unit, St Vincent's Hospital, Sydney

I will never forget it as long as I live.

This was the moment when I started to convince myself that if success was going to come my way, then it was going to be up to me. Paul Hanna himself. My older brother had just put his hand on my shoulder to tell me that the heart specialists, headed by world-renowned surgeons Dr Harry Windsor and Dr Victor Chang, were not confident that our dad was going to make it. I still remember it as if it were yesterday.

Waiting in the lobby, feeling vulnerable and scared, I watched in horror as the lift door opened to reveal a trolley carrying my father. With a sheet over him, and tubes and monitors connected to what looked like every part of his body, he was rushed into intensive care. There seemed to be about twenty doctors and nurses all tugging at different controls in a frantic effort to keep my dad alive.

I remember feeling angry and frustrated because I just had to sit there and accept the situation. I felt helpless. Then the realisation that my father was no longer going to be there hit me like a ton of bricks. My dad, who I thought would be with me till I was well into my adult years, was leaving me when I was just fourteen.

I felt every emotion that could be felt: anger, rejection, loneliness, but most of all, fear. And I had a conversation with myself that has stayed with me to this day. I remember deciding that my future was now up to me. That if I was going to make it, I would have to take total accountability for my success.

※   ※   ※

1

After dad died, my future looked pretty bleak. I was the son of immigrants, growing up in Sydney's western suburbs, and I had left school at the age of sixteen. I was on the razor's edge: either I was going to be successful at whatever career I chose, or I was going to go completely off the rails, as many teenagers do when faced with a trauma like this at such a tender age.

However, things changed one summer afternoon. I was in the city with some friends, shopping for Christmas presents, when I discovered a book that would change my life forever. *Think and Grow Rich*, by Napoleon Hill, was the most powerful kick in the pants I had ever had. All the encouragement and education I had been given up to then faded into the background. This was a blockbuster. This book convinced me that all successful people have had tremendous setbacks and it was these very setbacks that have made them successful.

After reading the book from cover to cover, I decided that no setback was ever going to beat me. From that point on, my life changed. From being an unemployed sixteen-year-old, I went on to a marketing career in the travel industry which allowed me not only to see the world back to front many times over, but to see it in grand style, first class all the way. All by the age of twenty-five.

Yes, it was 'pinch yourself' time. Here I was, designing the holidays Australians would take the following year, and it seemed that only five minutes ago I was a struggling teenager.

Up until my late twenties, I travelled the world and saw what is possible. I also discovered how fabulous Australia and Australians could be. I'm not ashamed to say that I love my country, and get a lump in my throat when I hear 'Waltzing Matilda'. But I thought to myself then, 'If we as a nation really hit our stride, the rest of the world wouldn't know what hit them'.

In a world where many countries are fighting each other because of ethnic and religious differences, most Australians are more interested in the latest cricket score or who you follow in football than in which god you worship. I saw a world where many nations still want to kill whales and dolphins, and yet in Australia, one mention of beached whales anywhere, any time, is sure to attract hundreds of helpers. And because of our isolation, we have had to keep abreast of what's happening worldwide, and therefore we have not become insular as many other nations have. But this isolation has also led to Australians not realising how great we could be.

As fate had it, I was whingeing once too often about this on a flight coming back to Australia. The businessman sitting next to me said, 'Why don't you stop whingeing and do something about it?' Like in the cartoons, a light bulb went on. Why not focus all my energy into assisting Australians to achieve more of their potential? On landing, I couldn't wait to get home to re-read *Think and Grow Rich* just one more time.

Life's a funny thing. Ten years after discovering this wonderful book my life had turned around completely. But the best was yet to come.

The following years saw my new business grow from giving free speeches at Rotary to working with the most senior businesspeople in the country. Thousands of people in corporate Australia have attended 'The Paul Hanna Seminar' in either half-day or full-day format, and many thousands more have heard me at their annual conference or convention. In the last few years, organisations have begun to realise that the partners of their employees are just as important as the people who work for them, so more and more of my seminars now have partners and families attending. The most recent growth in my business – proving just as rewarding as my seminars – is private consulting on a one-to-one basis with managers and staff from my client organisations.

I discover each day that every person who has achieved success in any area – be it financial or sporting, business or personal – has had to endure much more pain than the majority of the population. If physical pain is our wake-up call to get something in our body fixed, then other sorts of pain in our life must be seen in the same way. When you address the source of the pain, and fix it, it heals slowly and then you move on. If you keep putting it off, or keep placing bandages on top, the trouble-spot festers until it becomes unbearable.

Successful people understand pain. They know it's positive and a tool for success. They welcome pain into their life, because they know that when they deal with it, their self-esteem will soar and, with this, their ability to handle any future challenges.

The case studies you will read in this book are true stories (with names changed to protect the innocent!) told to me by people who have attended my seminars or consulted with me one-to-one. When I share the stories in my seminars, many people tell me they gain a lot from them. I know you, too, will find them to be of tremendous benefit.

＊ ＊ ＊

When I started my seminars, I made a decision to talk more about my audiences' lives – with all their trials, tribulations and aspirations – than about where I have come from. I wanted to give you this very brief summary about Paul Hanna so you can see that I was not born with a silver spoon in my mouth and that, like every other Australian, I have had my fair share of setbacks and successes.

My father died that afternoon in 1975. But with his death came the seed of persistence and determination: if I was going to achieve anything in my life, it was going to be up to me.

No excuses. No hard luck story. Just a determination to succeed and a belief that I CAN DO IT!

CHAPTER ONE

Attitude Is Everything!

'Things do not change; we change.'
HENRY DAVID THOREAU

IN THIS CHAPTER:

How your attitude controls your altitude in life

✳

How to change your autopilot, or opinion of yourself

✳

How your self-image or self-opinion controls
how high you fly

✳

How to control your cruising altitude in life

✳

How to use your past success for future challenges

✳

How you are in the pilot's seat of your life

✳

Why negative self-talk takes you to lower altitudes

✳

Why attitude is everything

The 747 is one of the twentieth century's greatest achievements. To this day, it remains the favourite aircraft of seasoned travellers because of its space, its technology and, more than anything else, its reliability. Survey after survey conducted around the world keeps rating the 747 as the most popular aircraft of all time.

But this book is not about planes. It's about how humans are designed in a similar way to the 747. In fact many of the concepts found in the 747 are really there as a result of how we think as human beings.

YOUR ATTITUDE DETERMINES YOUR ALTITUDE IN LIFE

Like the pilot of a 747, you have all the controls at your fingertips to allow you to take off and fly at any altitude you wish. But many people cruise along at the same altitude for years, unhappy with the bumpy ride they are experiencing in life, and thinking that they just have to put up with it.

Let me use what I call 'Jumbospeak' to illustrate how we all have the power to climb to any altitude, if only we take accountability for where we are at and know exactly where we want to go. It's very easy to say this, I know, but I want to demonstrate how you can lift yourself up to the next level of success or, in Jumbospeak, the *higher altitude*.

Let's say you are on board a 747 to London, cruising at 35 000 feet (10 000 metres). The computer which controls the height of the 747 is the 'autopilot'. It makes sure that the 747 never moves from its programmed altitude, which was set before takeoff.

Whenever the 747 starts to climb higher, the autopilot, like the cruise control in a car, sends electrical feedback telling the Jumbo to lower its height and get back to 35 000 feet. Conversely, when the 747 starts to fly lower, the autopilot sends electrical messages telling it to start lifting its game and fly higher. And on it goes, all the way to London.

En route to London, there are some tropical storms over Asia, and the plane has to fly higher to get over this rough patch. Singapore traffic control advises the pilots that they need to remain at the higher level for about ten minutes before descending back to their cruising altitude of 35 000 feet.

Because the change is required for a short period only, the pilots elect to fly the 747 up to the new altitude manually. Then, when they get clearance to return, they simply let go of the controls and the autopilot interrupts and takes over. The 747 returns to 35 000 feet, or the cruising altitude which was programmed before takeoff.

Your Opinion of Yourself Is Your Autopilot

Like the 747, you have been given beliefs at takeoff – except your takeoff was when you were a kid growing up. Whether you like it or not, you have been programmed in a similar way to the 747, and it is this programming that is keeping you cruising at the current altitude you are at in your life. If you leave your autopilot with the same information, the chances are that any changes in your life will be short-term ones.

Here's an example. Have you ever had more money in your bank account than usual? What happens after about a week? You go on a spending spree, which brings you back to your cruising altitude, or back to the programmed information about how much money you think you should have in your bank account.

Two Ways to Change How High You Fly

Like the 747 set on autopilot, any time you grab the controls of your life and try to change it, the results are only temporary. While you're holding the controls, you keep flying at that higher altitude, but as soon as you let go, your autopilot interrupts and takes you back down to your habitual cruising altitude.

If the pilots of the 747 wanted to fly higher than the pre-set altitude for the rest of their flight, they would have two choices: to keep hold of the controls all the way to London, thus overriding the autopilot, or to re-program the autopilot to the new altitude.

You face exactly the same challenge. To ensure that you stay at your new altitude, you must re-program your autopilot. And your autopilot is your *self-image*.

WHAT IS SELF-IMAGE?

Basically, self-image is how you see yourself – your opinion of yourself. All the beliefs you have accepted about yourself up to this point in your life make up your self-image.

Do you see yourself as a person who is confident and outgoing, or someone who is shy and scared of other people? Do you regard yourself as a positive person who sees the best in everyone you meet, or are you always focusing on the negative points of people?

Your self-image, or opinion of yourself, is basically what will eventually make or break you in life. What happens in life happens, and you can't change that. But what you *can* change is the way you look at life's events – how you evaluate them.

This concept can be compared to a pair of reading glasses. *You* decide how you view the world: you can choose either to do without the glasses and have limited vision, or to put them on and see everything more clearly. The world doesn't change whether or not you wear the glasses; it's only how you *look at* the world that changes.

Have a close look at the illustration on the next page and you will see very clearly how life is a self-fulfilling prophecy, that is, we get in life what we go looking for, good or bad.

You can see that, like the 747, you have an autopilot, which is your self-image. This then controls the altitude you fly at, which is the way you live your life.

To Fly Higher, the Autopilot Needs New Information

Essentially, when pilots give information to the autopilot to re-program it to a new altitude, they are effectively changing its belief system. With the new

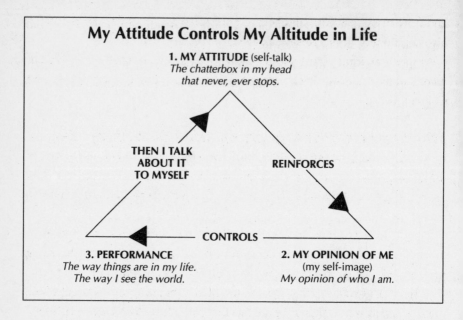

My Attitude Controls My Altitude in Life

1. MY ATTITUDE (self-talk)
*The chatterbox in my head
that never, ever stops.*

THEN I TALK
ABOUT IT
TO MYSELF

REINFORCES

CONTROLS

3. PERFORMANCE
*The way things are in my life.
The way I see the world.*

2. MY OPINION OF ME
(my self-image)
My opinion of who I am.

information, the autopilot knows that it has to fly the 747 at a higher altitude and keep it there, no matter what.

The same applies to your self-image. If you want to achieve a permanent change, you must re-program your opinion of yourself with new information. You are currently flying at the altitude you are because of the decisions you have made up to this point in your life. You need to be aware that if you keep on making the same decisions, things are not going to get much better, no matter how positive you are.

To change the direction you are heading in life, you have to make some tough decisions. Getting help to make those decisions could be the reason you picked up this book. If so, stick with me, because I have heaps of information that will assist you!

UNDERSTANDING CRUISING ALTITUDES
(Also Known as Comfort Zones)

Basically, your *cruising altitude* is what you are happy with in life – how much money you have in the bank, how many friends you think you need and how they treat you, and so on. Your relationship with your partner is also dictated by your cruising altitude.

As much as it may hurt you to know this, all the people in your life are attracted by yourself. There are no accidents. There is more on this in Chapter 10.

Why Changing Your Cruising Altitude Is Not Always Easy

At a certain stage of my seminar, I ask for a volunteer to get up in front of the class and summarise for ten minutes the last hour of my talk. I walk around the room looking as if I am going to pick someone, and everyone gets really tense.

People look around, hoping I will choose someone else and not them. Some pick up empty glasses to drink from, trying to distract me; some pretend they are preparing by writing notes; others just don't look at me.

When I let the room know that I am only joking, everyone lets out a sigh of relief and says how glad they are that they don't have to get up and present.

But what would happen if I took one of my attendees around Australia with me and asked them to do a ten-second introduction to every session? Initially they would be scared, but eventually they would start to get the hang of it. Their self-talk would start to change from 'I hate this' to 'This is getting really easy; I could get used to this'.

When you throw yourself into a new challenge without thinking, you will most probably bomb out. But if you prepare yourself via goal-setting, then your cruising altitude will slowly start to alter.

DECISION-MAKING AND YOUR CRUISING ALTITUDE

It is ultimately the decisions you make that will determine where you end up in life. We are all familiar with the decisions we make at work and home, such as 'I will go to lunch at 12 for one hour' or 'I will take the kids to Little Athletics tonight'. These are *conscious* decisions.

What I want to introduce here is the phenomenal power of your *subconscious* and the decisions that are made from this powerhouse.

How Past Conditioning Affects Your Decision-making

Pavlov, the Russian scientist, became famous with his 'dog trick'. He set up an experiment where he rang a bell, and if the dog came to him it was rewarded with a biscuit. After a couple of days, when the dog heard the bell it went straight to him, because it knew he would have a biscuit waiting.

After about a week, Pavlov discovered that the dog would start to salivate as soon as it heard the bell, because it was connecting the sound with food. It was thinking, 'When the bell rings, I'm getting fed!' Pavlov had conditioned the dog to expect food when it heard the sound of the bell.

Sometimes we act just like Pavlov's dog. Can you remember being asked to go to the principal's office when you were at school? What was the first thought that came into your mind? It was probably something like, 'What have I done now? I must be in trouble'. Usually that was the only reason you ever went to that office. Sometimes you *were* in trouble. But what about that time you arrived to find yourself asked to join a group of fellow students on Saturday to collect for the Red Cross!

This subconscious conditioning doesn't leave you once you've finished school. What would happen if you were asked to go straight to your boss's office on Friday morning, after a poor week of sales? Yes, the thoughts would run around your head like lottery balls: 'Oh no! I'm going to be sacked!' And you might decide to resign first. Then you arrive at the boss's office to see that he's having a farewell for Joe, who is leaving the company after ten years!

NEW INFORMATION MEANS NEW BELIEFS

Did you know there was a time when every person on Earth thought the world was flat? That if you travelled to the end of the Earth, you would fall off the edge? This was the common belief until Christopher Columbus decided that he had enough facts to prove that the world was in fact round, and that if you did sail to 'the edge', you wouldn't fall off, but would keep on sailing back to where you started.

'The world is round,' he declared, 'not flat!' Of course, no one believed this ridiculous statement, especially when no ship had yet sailed to 'the edge' to prove his point. Certainly, Columbus had not. Why should they believe him? What proof did he have? History now records that Columbus not only broke one of the most widely held beliefs ever entertained by humans, but discovered another world in the process.

'No Human Being Can Run the Mile in Less than Four Minutes'

The Ancient Greeks and Romans tried for centuries to break the barrier of the four-minute mile. No one had ever run the mile in less than four minutes. It couldn't be done. 'Humanly impossible', said the experts. The Romans even had lions chase men to see if this would give them a hurry-up. Sadly for the human guinea pigs, it didn't work.

The four-minute barrier stayed unbroken until a young Englishman named Roger Bannister decided he was going to do it. Bannister smashed the unbreakable when on 6 May 1954 he ran the mile in 3 minutes 59.6 seconds. He was hailed as a hero and later received a knighthood.

The breaking of the record was a fantastic feat, but the reason I'm sharing this story is to tell you what happened afterwards, which I think is even more important and fascinating. Over the next four years more than forty people ran the mile in less than four minutes. The 'unbreakable' was now being broken quite regularly. The belief had been changed: 'You can now run the mile in less than four minutes'. Permission granted!

What Four-minute Mile Barrier Do You Have to Break?

As you can see by these two very famous instances of belief-breaking, *what you believe you can do* can severely hamper your progress at work and in your personal life – or it can help you to reach amazing goals.

In a sense, we all have to run the four-minute mile every day, because just going to work and doing our best possible job means challenging some of the beliefs we currently hold about the job we are in. How many times a day do you use limiting statements or hear them used around the office or at home? Here are a few that you might relate to:

Work

'That's the way it's always been done.'
'You won't get anywhere by rocking the boat.'

13

'When I was your age, blah blah blah blah . . .'
'Women will never get ahead in this company.'
'You need a degree to get ahead in this world today.'
'It's not *what* you know in this organisation, it's *who* you know.'

Home
'You're just like your old man – untidy!'
'Why can't you be more like your older brother?'
'You'll go nowhere with that attitude.'
'The middle child always struggles.'
'The youngest is always spoilt.'

No Blaming Parents from Here on in

The most important part of changing is realising that you have the power to do it; realising that your parents did the best they could with what they had, but now it's over to you. No more excuses. Total accountability.

In my consulting, it's amazing how many people have said to me that they realise now that they have been blaming their parents for things that happened long ago, when instead they could have been re-programming their autopilot or self-image with new information.

YOUR SELF-TALK CONTROLS YOUR SELF-IMAGE

As you can see in the diagram on page 10, how you talk to yourself is the key to keeping self-image pumping along. Positive thinking is a waste of time if you only do it selectively and occasionally. For self-talk to be of benefit you must learn to control it all the time, so that your opinion of yourself remains consistent.

The most amazing thing about your self-image is that *you* make the decision to either lift it or lower it. No one else can do this. How you talk to yourself on a day-to-day basis determines how your autopilot is programmed, and how high you fly in life.

Replaying Mental Videos

Did you know that you think in pictures? The way you speak to yourself triggers mental pictures of how you see yourself, and this controls how you feel emotionally.

Can you remember the last time you rented a video that was 'ordinary'? How long did the viewing last? Well, that probably depended on whether you had something better to watch. For example, if a football decider match or the men's or women's final at Wimbledon was on, you wouldn't waste your time watching some second-rate video.

That's exactly how we think as human beings. When we make a mistake, we talk to ourselves about it and start to 'replay the video' of the mistake. We start to get visual images of failure and talk ourselves down to a lower altitude. Things start to get a bit bumpy, and we ask why. We start to blame the people and events around us for how we feel, when in fact it was *our* decision to replay the video which made us feel bad. But if we had a better video to watch, that is, some visual images of success, we wouldn't do this.

Think of your favourite video. How do you feel when it finishes? Do you feel motivated and excited? Happy and relaxed? When we replay a positive event in our mind, it has the same effect as replaying a 'positive' video. We tell ourselves how great we feel and start self-talking in a positive way.

TALK YOURSELF UP TO SUCCESS

One of the most consistent messages in any self-development manual is that the way you speak to yourself will eventually decide how well you go in life.

Can you remember a time when things weren't going well for you? If someone asked you how you were doing, your reply was something like 'Lousy' or 'Not bad', in a downbeat tone. Not only did this tell the other person that you weren't feeling great, but it reinforced to *you* how bad you felt – and the cycle continued, just like in the diagram on page 10.

By controlling your self-talk, *you* decide how you want to view life. Think about how often you say bad things about yourself, things like: 'You idiot – what made you do that?' or 'I'm so fat/ugly'. You wouldn't have many friends if you spoke to them the way you speak to yourself!

On a piece of paper, make a list of the negative self-talk statements you find yourself commonly using. No one is going to read this, so be honest with yourself. When you have written as many as you can think of, try to match each negative statement with a positive statement that you could use instead. The next time you find yourself using a negative statement, challenge your self-talk and replace the statement with a positive one. I've given you a few examples to start you off.

Negative Self-talk Statement	Positive Self-talk Statement
I'm exhausted.	I feel great.
I'm sick of this job.	I like my job more and more every day.
The world stinks.	I love life.

Make a commitment *now* to start speaking with upbeat words when carrying on a conversation with yourself or your family and friends. We all move in the direction of our current thoughts, so where you are is no accident. You planned it. You decided to be there. You knowingly or unknowingly planned to be there. But you can also change the direction of your life – if you want to!

Many years ago, while travelling in the United States, I was waiting in an airport lounge when I stumbled across this poem in a magazine. I believe it sums up fully how accountable we all are for our own successes – and failures.

Attitude
The longer I live, the more I realise
the impact of attitude on life.

It is more important than education,
than money, than circumstances,
than failures, than successes,
than whatever anyone might say or do.

It is more important
than appearances, giftedness or skill.
The remarkable thing is that
we have the choice to create
the attitude we have for that day.

We cannot change our past.
We cannot change the way people act.
We cannot change the inevitable.

The one thing we can change
is the only thing we have control over,
and that is our attitude.

I'm convinced that life is
10 per cent what actually happens to us,
and 90 per cent how we react to it.

You have total choice when it comes to how you feel. No ifs or buts. You are in the pilot's seat!

WANT TO KNOW MORE ABOUT . . . ?	Turn to . . .
How to lift your opinion of yourself	Chapter 2
Attracting the good things in life	Chapter 13
How the past might be holding you back	Chapter 9
Visualising more success in your life	Chapter 4
Taking more accountability for your success	Chapter 4
Using SuccessSpeak to climb to the next altitude	Chapter 6
Locus of Control and the next altitude	Chapter 2

CHAPTER TWO

Self-confidence – It's the Key

'Sow a thought and you reap an act;
Sow an act and you reap a habit;
Sow a habit and you reap a character;
Sow a character and you reap a destiny.'

RALPH WALDO EMERSON

IN THIS CHAPTER:

How to improve your self-confidence

✳

No one can upset you unless you give them permission

✳

How winners come back from defeat

✳

How your opinion of yourself determines your success

✳

Why the world is your mirror

✳

Mind poisoning and negative people

✳

Taking full accountability for your success

✳

How to improve your kids' self-esteem

✳

Self-esteem and your partner

✳

How to be strong during the tough times

✳

How mixing with positive people creates success

One of the best quotes I have ever heard about self-image, or self-esteem, is 'We compare our inners to other people's outers'. If you compare yourself to the people around you, you will never really grow in self-esteem. So how do you know if you have high or low self-esteem?

Well, while you can get cholesterol tests at chemists and blood tests at the doctor, the test for self-esteem is how you feel about you. No one can jump into your head and feel how you feel. Sure, there are hundreds of self-esteem evaluations you can put yourself through, but in the end, it's your own opinion that really matters.

There is a very simple way to get an idea of how self-esteem works and how you are going at the moment. I call it the 'Self-esteem Bank Account'.

YOUR SELF-ESTEEM BANK ACCOUNT

This account works pretty much like your bank savings account, in that you can deposit or withdraw at will. And like every bank account, when you spend too much you overdraw, resulting in your account going into the red. Also like your bank account, you are the only one with the PIN number. In other words, only you can deposit or withdraw.

Let's get even more specific: no one else can upset you! Now before you think I am living in a dream world, I'll explain how powerful this statement really is. We often give the power of controlling our self-esteem to the people around us – mothers, fathers, husbands, wives, even the kids – instead of making a conscious effort to be vigilant regarding what is said to us and what we are prepared to accept. Of course you are going to get cheesed off sometimes, but you have to give the okay before someone can upset you. *You have to give them permission.*

You also have to give permission to let compliments have any positive effect on your Self-esteem Bank Account – that is, you have to accept the compliments. We are all ready to accept a kick in the pants, but we tend to be very wary when someone offers us a compliment. We might even say, 'I wonder what *he* wants?' and be very suspicious.

Let's go back to the bank account analogy. What happens when you get some unexpected bills in the mail? You're not thrilled about them, but you still have to pay them. Your bank balance might not look as healthy as it did before you paid the bills, but you still have money in your account for any unexpected withdrawals. Your Self-esteem Bank Account works in pretty much the same way. If you can build your balance up regularly, you will find that when you come face to face with setbacks, they will pass without rocking your foundations.

THE MAN IN THE MIRROR

Greg 'The Shark' Norman, Australia's and the world's number one golfer, once said that when he was not performing up to his own standards, and the press were hounding him, he always knew that the advice that would get him out of trouble would be that of 'The Man in the Mirror'.

On Australian television, Greg was asked how he had pulled himself out of the slump that preceded his triumphant win in the 1993 British Open. He replied that he had lifted his game bit by bit, hole by hole. Before every tournament he would set a small, realistic goal. For example, his goal might be to do really well at Hole 9 – he wasn't aiming to win the whole tournament, just to do really well in one part of it. After it was over, he may not have won the tournament, but he knew he had 'won' what he set out to win.

It's interesting to note that the sports media at that time kept on with their usual 'Norman fails' lines without really knowing what was happening in this champion's mind. History now records Greg Norman as not only

Australia's leading golfer, not only the world's leading golfer, but in financial terms, one of the most successful sportspeople ever.

So, who is the Shark's 'Man in the Mirror'? About six years ago, I was on a speaking tour of Australia with one of the largest insurance companies in the country, doing sessions with about 1000 people from the organisation. At the end of the tour, a woman named Suzanne came up and congratulated me for what she said was a very moving and thought-provoking two hours. She asked, 'Paul, have you seen "The Man in the Mirror"?'

My mind instantly flashed to the Greg Norman interview. I said I had heard of it, but no, I had not seen it. Suzanne told me it was found in a death-row prison in the USA. Two prisoners were about to be executed. In the morning, after their last meal, they were taken from the cell where they had been housed for the night. When the prison guards came to clean up the cell later, they found 'The Man in the Mirror' inscribed on the wall.

I returned from the tour to find this on my fax machine from Suzanne:

The Man in the Mirror

If you get what you want in your struggle for self
And the world makes you King for a day
Then go to the mirror and look at yourself
And see what that Man has to say

For it isn't a man's father, mother or wife
Whose judgement upon him must pass
The fellow whose verdict counts most in his life
Is the Man staring back from the glass

He's the fellow to please, never mind all the rest
For he's with you clear up to the end
And you've passed your most dangerous, difficult test
If the Man in the glass is your friend

You can fool the whole world down the pathway of years
And get pats on the back as you pass
But your final reward will be heartache and tears
If you've cheated the Man in the glass

I remember the first time I read this poem. I had to read it again and again. To me, it really is the foundation of self-esteem.

THE WORLD IS YOUR MIRROR

Wow! Is that what you thought when you read 'The Man in the Mirror'? I know that's what I thought. It's such a powerful piece, and conveys in a subtle way three very important points:

1. *You* have to like yourself before anyone else will.
2. Who cares what other people think about you? It's the opinion you hold of yourself that really counts.
3. You can fool some of the people some of the time, but in the end you can't fool yourself.

I love sharing this poem in my seminars because of the different ways people react to it. I have always received a positive response, but on one occasion I was asking for my audience's reaction and a guy in his thirties put up his hand. He said, 'I really enjoyed 'The Man In The Mirror', because it explains something that has puzzled me for quite a while'.

David went on to say that he used to work for a very successful businessman. 'Every morning the boss would stroll through the office to say g'day. When he got to me he would always make some sort of remark that was uplifting and positive. One morning he came through our department and said, "David, do you know the person you shaved this morning?" I was stunned. I thought, "I didn't shave anyone this morning! What's he talking about?"

'He kept on asking me, and I became more curious. When I asked him what he meant, he simply replied, "One day you will find out" '. David said that after he read 'The Man in the Mirror' at my seminar, his boss's riddle had finally been solved.

WHAT DOES IT TAKE TO UPSET YOU?

Do you ever wake up in the morning and realise you've slept really badly? You've tossed and turned, and kept waking up. Finally, when morning arrives, you feel like you've had no sleep. After a slow start, you get into the car to drive to work. You're on the road when suddenly someone hangs a left without indicating, just missing the front of your car. What would most people do in this situation? 'You !!@#$% idiot!' You bet, and so would I!

Let's take another scenario. You've had a great night's sleep and everything seems to be running okay. You get up in time to have some breakfast; you take your time, listening to your favourite radio program. Everything is looking good. Suddenly, when you're driving, this guy cuts you off in the traffic. What would be the difference in your reaction? You would probably just signal to let the driver in, or think 'Okay, mate, get in. I have my eyes on bigger things'.

Have you ever heard someone in your office or family say that they have a 'short fuse'? They lose their temper easily and often. But there is really no such thing as a short temper — it's low self-esteem.

I once heard a brilliant statement that, to me, sums this up beautifully: *'The size of a person is determined by what it takes to upset them'*. The person who 'loses it' easily is really saying that they are upset by the little things in life. Can you imagine what's happening to their Self-esteem Bank Account? Every time they get upset they are withdrawing self-esteem from their account and flying lower and lower. The lower they get, the more upset they get. The more upset they get, the more they blame, and around in circles they go.

Take some time now to write down the things that have upset you in the past two weeks. Have a look at your list. Were the things that upset you big things or little things? Can you see where you could remain a bit more in control? When I do this exercise, I recognise certain signals which tell me if my Self-esteem Bank Account is getting depleted or running low. For example, I might find that when I've checked in to a hotel or airport, little things like delays or talkative people have upset me. When I'm feeling good, I can switch off and ignore the chatterboxes or screaming kids by listening to the in-flight audio. Or if a flight is delayed, I might phone a client or two and see how their business and staff are going.

> # We can't control the direction of the wind, but we can adjust our sails.

I remember seeing the above quote about seven years ago at a sailing club in Singapore. To me, it says it all about coping in today's rapidly changing environment. If you constantly let little things upset you, you really have no hope of ever lifting your Self-esteem Bank Balance to any significant level. You will always be making withdrawals because of events you have allowed to upset you.

It's not the events, or the comments people make about you, that cause you to be upset – it's how you interpret them. You, and only you, make the decision whether to withdraw from or deposit into your Self-esteem Bank Account.

MIND POISONING IS LIKE FOOD POISONING

Have you ever had food poisoning? If not, I am sure you have witnessed a relative or friend going down with some bug that causes their whole body to go into total 'rejection' mode. Whenever I have an upset stomach, I am reminded of the power of my subconscious mind – always there to protect and preserve me at all costs. Your subconscious works in the same way as your digestive system, but instead of protecting you against a negative *physical* infection, it protects you against another kind of infection: negative *thinking*, or 'mind poisoning'.

So how do you protect your thinking from being infected by negativity? Like your digestive system, you need to have a system in place that protects you at all times.

Let's go back to the 747. Can you imagine how rough flying would be if pilots did not have advance-warning systems to let them know what's ahead? If you have ever flown, you will have noticed the seat-belt sign flash on *before* it starts to get bumpy. You might have questioned why you needed the belt when everything seemed okay. Then suddenly, you weren't guessing any more. The plane started to shake a little, and then as quickly as it started, it stopped. Now you're glad that seat-belt sign came on!

Just like the 747, you need advance warnings in your life.

The Ride to Work

Steve, a computer analyst, shared a very enlightening story with me. He said that the previous year he had been offered the opportunity to attend a middle-management seminar at an outside facility. Eager to improve his education, Steve accepted. Later that week he received a phone call from Harry, a manager in another department who had also been nominated to attend the seminar.

Harry rang to advise Steve that he would be attending and asked if Steve would like to travel with him to and from the venue, as they both lived in the same southern suburb and the seminar was in North Sydney.

Steve accepted Harry's offer with thanks. Because the distance was at least one hour in each direction, the two men had a lot of time to chat and discuss the company. But Harry was one of those people whose conversation mainly consists of 'knocking' things. After two days of commuting, Steve said that he noticed he had started to think like Harry.

At first, Harry's negative comments hadn't really bothered Steve, but after hearing them over and over again, Steve said that he began to worry, because he started to think that some of what Harry said had merit. The constant 'knocking' of everything was starting to rub off. Steve didn't want to be a 'knocker', so he decided to do something about it. He told Harry that he would drive himself for the rest of the week and thanked him for driving for the last two days. Steve went on to tell me that he had not realised how powerfully other people's thinking could affect his own.

He knew he was 'in the driver's seat of his life', and he also knew that no one could touch his Self-esteem Bank Account unless he gave permission. But even knowing all that, he had still found himself agreeing with Harry and then starting to think like him – after only two days.

What Happens if You Live with a 'Harry'?

One of the most common questions I get regarding self-esteem, especially from people who are married or in a relationship, is 'What happens if I am married to a negative person like Harry?', or words to that effect.

In a recent seminar for a large company, one of the most senior managers sat next to me at lunch. Christine said that every time she comes home from a seminar like mine she is fired up and ready to commit to a new set of goals, both corporately and personally. But when she attempts to talk to her husband Brad, a plumber, he says, 'Oh, you've been to one of those pump-up sessions again. You know it will never last'. Christine said that, despite what Brad says, she knows the reason she has managed to climb the corporate ladder is because her company is always sending its managers off to seminars, 'always making sure we stay on top of things'.

'But the irony is', she said, 'Brad is the one that needs this stuff the most. He is always whingeing that the market is too tough and that he can't get enough business, and then in the next breath he says that his customers are never satisfied'.

The growth in my 'partner' seminars is proof that people want to improve not only their corporate life but also their personal life. As things turned out, Christine's company put on a partners' seminar and her husband came along. After the seminar she introduced me to a very excited and enthusiastic Brad. He said that he had enjoyed the seminar immensely and realised now what Christine was carrying on about when she came home from my original seminar.

Brad said that the point that most struck him was that he was trying to run his business with no clear set of goals, and that both he and Christine needed to reset their personal goals.

DO YOUR BANKING DAILY

For many of us, day-to-day life is going to work and then coming home, wishing that things would improve but not really knowing how to achieve this. Before any improvement occurs, you have to focus on your Self-esteem Bank Account.

In a recent partners' seminar for a major Australian bank (Which bank? No, not that one!), Linda explained how, for years, she had waited for her husband, Roger, to get home from work and ask her how things had gone during her day. Instead, he would come home, exhausted from the grind at his stockbroking business, and plonk himself in front of the TV. Linda said that she felt she needed Roger to care about her as much as he did about his business. When he showed no interest in her life, her self-esteem dropped further and further, until one day she read a self-help book which focused on taking accountability for your own self-esteem levels and not blaming others. She realised that her self-esteem was at the level it was because she was waiting for someone else to go to her Self-esteem Bank Account and make some deposits. She made a determined effort from that day on not to blame Roger for her unhappiness. She started to take full responsibility for herself.

LOCUS OF CONTROL

How many people do you know right now who think, like Linda used to, that the reason they are where they are is because of someone else's actions?

'Locus of Control' strikes at the heart of this. 'Locus' is Latin for 'position', so Locus of Control is simply where you think the position of control is in your life. The more you think the Locus of Control resides with you, the easier it will be for you to see how to improve your performance. If you think the Locus of Control of your life is with other people or events, you give those people or events the power to walk right over you.

How much Locus of Control are you currently taking for your situation in life? Most people's Locus of Control is 100 per cent with them when they are at work, where they take total accountability for events and how to handle them. But when these people get home, they give away their power to events or people around them.

Sharon, a personal assistant for a senior businessman in Melbourne, shared the following scenario. She knew that, as Rick's PA, the buck stopped with her as far as his diary went. He was constantly on the move, travelling around Australia, but she always managed achieve the balance of fitting in all his appointments while at the same time leaving him enough free time to catch up.

But Sharon said that she had always wondered why at work she was very precise and successful, yet at home felt she was the opposite. At home, she was always making decisions that collided with each other. No one seemed to be happy, and there were always little upsets. Then Sharon discovered Locus of Control and taking accountability. While she was having great success at work, at home she was letting events control her.

Sharon said that for a long time she has wanted to hold the Christmas family lunch at her place, instead of at her younger brother's home where it has been for the last twenty years. Christmas at her brother's has always been enjoyable, but never very exciting. And, Sharon said, his wife never stops complaining about how she has been preparing since August! Every time Sharon offers to hold the next Christmas lunch, her mother steps in and says, 'This is the way it's always been since your brother got married'.

Sharon said that as soon as her mother speaks, that's it. She finds herself saying, 'Oh well, if mum wants it that way . . .', and giving in for yet another year.

But this Christmas, lunch is over at Sharon's! What happened? What changed? One thing, and one thing only. Sharon took total accountability to convince everyone that just this once, it would be great to have a change. Just for one year. She was determined that the next Christmas would be over at her place. Like she would have done at work, Sharon sat down with her husband and focused on every negative comment they had heard over the years and, without being negative or condescending, role-played to themselves the answers they would give.

When they broke the news, there was a lot of hot air and the usual 'Not this again!' comments. But Sharon and her husband convinced everyone that for next Christmas a change would be exciting, and something to look forward to.

Sharon told me that the most amazing thing was this: after they had got the okay from everyone, her mother came up to her, full of praise for how well Sharon had handled all the objections, and said she was looking forward to next Christmas. And her sister-in-law who was always complaining said how thrilled she was to have a break 'for once'!

Now I am not for one moment saying that you should go around on your high horse telling others to lift their game. More the opposite: just go about your life quietly and let them see for themselves. If other people see you being accountable for your own life and your own self-esteem, they will be encouraged to do the same.

RAISING YOUR KIDS' SELF-ESTEEM

In the last five years, not a seminar has passed without someone coming up to me during the break and letting me know how they have had success with their young children or teenagers using my material.

Karen, a nurse, was attending with her husband, a luxury-car salesman whose dealership had decided to have a partners' seminar. Karen came up to me during the morning tea break and said she had learnt the hard way how self-esteem can really make or break a child's performance. Her son from a previous marriage, Jason, was having trouble at school and finding it hard to settle down. The toll of the difficult separation from her ex-husband was starting to show in Jason's performance at school. He had tantrums if he didn't get his own way, and was constantly disruptive in class. It was the same at home.

But one day there was a sudden change in Jason's behaviour. His room, which up till then had always been a pig sty, was much tidier. Curious to find out the reason for this, Karen spoke to Jason's teacher, Sarah. Sarah explained to Karen that she had been at her wits' end with him; she had tried every kind of discipline but Jason was not responding. As she had nothing to lose, she decided to use reverse psychology and instead of always telling Jason what he was doing wrong, she started giving him jobs that were usually only given to the best-behaved student. Sarah said it was like a bolt of lightning had struck. From that moment, Jason's performance started to improve, and he began to settle down. The change Karen had noticed at home meant that Jason was striving for the same recognition from his family as he was receiving at school.

What happened? Was there a bolt of lightning? I don't think so. There is only one reason for the change in Jason's behaviour: his Self-esteem Bank Account was starting to be topped up again. After his mother's separation and divorce, he was surrounded by negativity and this was being played out in everything he did. By treating him with respect at school, his teacher had helped him to start looking at things in a positive way instead.

The Chinese have a great saying, 'Running water flows downhill', which simply means that whatever is happening above in the family is sure to flow down to the kids. Likewise, whatever is happening in the boardroom in your organisation will eventually filter down to the staff.

If you have a problem kid at home, try Jason's teacher's method and see how you get on. I know when I share this story in my seminars it gets a lot of reaction, and many couples write and thank me for getting them through what has usually been a very trying period. They realise that the problems in their relationship have been filtering down to their kids, and that if they can get their act together, then maybe the kids will start to turn around.

Jason is seven, but I think the same concept works for people of all ages. We are all really just big kids in grown-up clothes, striving to be told that we are going well, that what we are achieving in life is worthwhile, and that we are important.

BIGGER THINGS TO FOCUS ON

The following story shows how, when you focus on the big picture, the little things stop being a problem. Quite often, I have couples who work in the same organisation attending the same seminar. Darren and Michelle are one such couple.

Both worked for the same multinational company and had been there for about seven years. They had met through mutual friends and dated each other for a couple of years before they married. For the first two years or so of their marriage, they had constantly gone out with friends and had a great time. Later, all these friends – who had married around the same time as they had – started to have kids. Things changed. Social events began to be centred around the kids.

While both Darren and Michelle wanted to start a family eventually, they were keen to establish themselves financially and emotionally before they took the plunge into parenthood. As their social scene came to a screaming halt in front of them, they discovered how little they really knew each other. With no distractions such as parties and weekends away with friends, they suddenly came to the realisation that they now had to be each other's best friend. Although they had believed their relationship was equal to or better than that of most of their friends, they now realised that the Self-esteem Bank Account for their relationship was in fact running pretty low. Their aims had become blurred and they were finding it hard to focus their energy and love.

Six months passed and I bumped into Darren at another conference. He looked relaxed and told me that his and Michelle's relationship was blooming like never before. When I asked what was the most important thing they had done as a couple to lift their relationship, Darren said they had learnt how to be aware of each other's self-esteem, and had made every effort to assist each other in increasing their Self-esteem Bank Account. 'For instance, when we first met we were constantly complimenting each other on the smallest things – like what the other person was wearing or doing. We had let this slip. And we used to go out at least once a week after work and take in a movie. This had somehow slipped through, too. Without these things our level of self-esteem had gone down'.

Darren commented how the little things that had been upsetting both of them still happened, but no longer had an impact on their relationship – because they did not allow those incidents power. Compared to the bigger picture of where they wanted to go, these small upsets remained small: 'We've got bigger things to focus on', said Darren. 'We started to look forward and plan where we wanted to be two years from now. We know that kids are going to figure in the picture somewhere, but we're still not sure when. What we do know is that we want to go to Europe and India before the kids come along, so that is the big goal we have set for the next twelve months'.

GETTING THROUGH THE BAD TIMES WITH YOUR PARTNER

Anne Morrow Lindbergh, in her brilliant book *Gift from the Sea*, compares life to the ocean: everything in life is cyclical, just like the tide. Success comes in and then goes out, comes in and goes out. Your health comes in, goes out, comes in ...

Think of your relationship with your partner. Can you remember a truly great period when everything was going fantastically? You were getting on really well, and nothing could faze either of you. I'm sure you can also remember dark times, times when nothing you said could make the other person happy. You'd say, 'But what am I doing wrong?' and they'd reply, 'It's not you, it's me'. Sound familiar?

These times are when your own level of self-esteem and confidence comes to the rescue. You know that your own self-esteem is intact, and you have to realise that it's not you that's the problem. Have the courage to give the other person some space to sort themselves out. As tempting as it may seem, don't try to solve their problems for them – this takes away their power. They are the only one who can raise their Self-esteem Bank Account Balance. The important point here is this: if you do not let them have their space, your own self-esteem could start to be affected by their negativity.

You can't change the world by yourself. If you know someone who is slipping backwards, for whatever reason, give them the support they need while they are trying to find themselves. Subtly leave self-development literature around the house that will tempt them to want to find out more. Remember, you are 'selling' here, and no one likes to be sold to but everyone likes to buy. And people buy benefits – sell the sizzle, not the sausage!

What's in it for them if they go to a seminar? Or read a book? Or listen to a tape? Sell the benefits not only for them but for you, too.

MENTORING – MIX WITH PEOPLE YOU WANT TO BECOME LIKE

Later in this book you will read how you move towards whatever it is you are thinking about. One of the quickest ways you can start to change your thinking so as to look at life in a more positive way is to mix with people who think that way. If you hang around with people who are successful, their positive outlook will well and truly rub off on you.

Have dinner with a winner and you will find that no matter what the discussion is about, it is always goal-oriented. Winners never blame others for their situation; they are always looking forward and chasing results. They take accountability for where they are at and where they want to go.

Whenever we hear in the media of a teenager committing a crime, inevitably a counsellor or foster parent, or even the real parents, admit that somehow, some way, their son fell into the wrong crowd and whammo! Now his whole life has been tarnished.

What's the difference between a teenager hanging around the wrong crowd and committing a crime and a thirty-seven-year-old accountant getting drunk every afternoon with his mates at the pub? It's the same thing. The bond between the teenager and his fellow thugs and the accountant and his mates leads to the same end.

> # You control who you
> # hang around with.

Who are you hanging around with? Who shapes the way you feel about you? Do they constantly put you down? Do they always make you the butt of jokes?

Take a good, long, hard look at who you call your friends and you might be surprised just how much they are holding you back from achieving more. While I would be the first person to say that they are not doing it maliciously, that's not the point. The point is this: if you were really to get your act together and start to achieve big things, you might find that some of the people around you would feel threatened. Subconsciously, they go into 'hold-back mode' to make sure that you don't start to believe you can do better – because they think that, if you start to climb, they could lose you as a friend. You will have to be the judge here, but remember: our most dominant thoughts control where we end up.

Success

If you think you are beaten, you are.
If you think you dare not you don't.
If you like to win, but you think you can't,
It is almost certain you won't.

If you think you'll lose, you're lost
For out of the world we find,
Success begins with a person's will
It's all in the state of mind.

If you think you are outclassed, you are,
You've got to think high to rise,
You've got to be sure of yourself before
You can ever win a prize.

Life's battles don't always go
To the stronger or faster person,
But sooner or later the person who wins
Is the person who thinks they can!

CHAPTER THREE

Luck and How to Attract It

'Chance favours the prepared mind.'
LOUIS PASTEUR

IN THIS CHAPTER:

How clarity of purpose creates luck

✹

Why you first have to decide what you want

✹

How you screen out 'junk' information

✹

When you play the lottery, you delay luck

✹

How 'mind-blinkers' work against more success

✹

How you are *always* 'in the right place
at the right time'

✹

Why impatience implies self-doubt

T hese days, it seems that every second advertisement on TV is bombarding us with 'Get rich quick' messages: 'Get your ticket for Mother's Day Millions!' 'Your chance to win a Father's Day Fortune!' And on it goes.

Ads like this promise to give us that vital ingredient we think comes from outside of us – luck. And we flock to these promises because they are the only form of luck we've heard about. For many people, 'luck' is something that happens when they win a prize or perhaps some money. The media reinforce this message with promises of how all our dreams will come true on Monday night if we just buy a ticket.

WINNERS KNOW THAT THEY CREATE THEIR OWN LUCK

What could you achieve if you made a decision never again to buy any sort of lottery ticket? What if you decided that the only 'luck' you were going to have would come from *within you*? All successful people know that they create their own luck – that they put themselves in the right place at the right time.

My version of luck is best explained by the following diagram. Whenever I show it to someone successful, they agree with it totally. They know it's true because it has worked in their life. When you focus all your energies and thinking towards a goal, the opportunities start to happen, as if on cue.

LUCK
is the crossroads of opportunity and preparation!

Search Party Cells

Imagine you're off to do your weekly grocery shopping at the super-market. What's the first thing you start to think of as you approach the supermarket entrance? A parking space, of course. And what never seems to be there? A parking space!

Then suddenly you 'get lucky'. You start to notice people walking towards their cars with bags full of groceries. Then you notice the white lights on the rear of cars which are reversing out of their parking spaces. You may even see the exhaust fumes of someone's car as they start it up in readiness to reverse and leave.

As soon as you clarify what you want, the 'Search Party Cells' in your mind start to search for answers. Decide 'parking space', and guess what?

You start to notice everything to do with parking spaces. It's got nothing to do with luck!

Here's another example. You go to the video store knowing that you *must* return home with a video because some friends are coming over that night to watch TV. The big question in your mind is, 'Which video will I get?' You walk around the video store for about forty-five minutes searching for a suitable video – and then what happens? You can't decide on one, and get pretty cheesed off with yourself. Frustrated by your lack of success, you decide you had better make a decision. You choose a video you have all seen before and return home with it. When you put it in your video player and your friends see what you have brought home, all hell breaks loose. 'We've seen this before! Why did you get this?! Couldn't you get anything better?'

One of your more empathetic friends mentions that she saw a fabulous new-release video last week. You don't remember seeing this particular video on the shelves when you were in the video store, but tell her that next time you're there you will look out for it.

When you go to the store the next morning, what's on the right as soon as you enter? One hundred copies of that new release! Was it there yesterday? You bet – all 100 copies. Why didn't you see them? Lack of clarity. Once your goal is clear and focused, you will see how to reach it.

Begin with the End in Mind

Everyone has had the experience of going shopping for a birthday present for a friend but returning home three hours later frustrated, because you couldn't find anything decent.

But what about the person you went shopping with, who, unlike you, knew exactly what he was going to get – let's say a CD of the birthday girl's favourite artist, Harry Connick Jr. How long did it take him to purchase the CD? About five minutes, at the most. He started with his end in mind, that is, to get a Harry Connick CD, and as soon as he entered the shopping centre he made a beeline for the music store, then the jazz section, then the letter C for Connick. Bingo! The CD is purchased.

Was your friend 'lucky'? No. He had a clear idea of what he wanted, and his Search Party Cells showed him how to get it.

43

I Thought I Had a Unique Car!

You're looking for a new car and you see one that is an unusual colour. You convince yourself that you have to have this car because the colour is unique – it's one of a kind. Twenty-four hours after you have bought the car, you have seen about twenty other cars on the road that look exactly like yours. They are all the same 'unique' colour.

Salespeople call this phenomenon 'buyer's remorse'. You need to prove to yourself that you have made a wise decision, so your Search Party Cells start to look for proof. What it also demonstrates is that when you focus your thinking, it's amazing what you start to see around you.

MIND-BLINKERS

Most Australians are familiar with the fabulous atmosphere of a summer's day spent at the beach – waves crashing, kids playing games and screaming at the tops of their voices, helicopters doing shark checks, surf-rescue boats on patrol and music coming from loudspeakers.

But have you noticed that as soon as you pick up a newspaper or book and start to read it, all the noise seems to become blocked out as you focus on what you are reading?

Melissa, the mother of two sets of twins, came up at one of my seminars and told me that blocking out the noise is the only way she has managed to stay sane. When the kids are playing games and screaming, the house is a mess, and she feels at the end of her tether, she sits herself down on the couch, picks up a magazine and loses herself in it for half an hour. She said that those thirty minutes are the difference between losing her temper with the twins (and her husband when he arrives home), and remaining focused and in control.

Because my job takes me around Australia on a regular basis, plane travel is a part of my life. I love it, and get a real buzz every time I board a plane. The down side, of course, is that I can never predict whether that 'passenger from hell' will be sitting next to me for the four-hour trip from Sydney to Perth. Or if that six-month-old baby who was using its lungs so well in the terminal will be in the row behind me.

To keep my sanity (and also to relax) in these situations, I put on my headset and listen to some classical music on the inflight entertainment. I am not, in fact, a big classical-music fan, but for this purpose it gives me something to focus on and helps quieten my mind. When I put on the music, all the engine noise, screaming kids and sounds of the cabin crew doing meal service are screened out. I am in the pilot's seat of my life. I decide what upsets me.

Sydney's Third Runway

Who could ever forget the protests and delays that occurred when Sydney's third runway was opened? Even though I just about live on planes, I have total empathy for the occupants of houses under any flight path.

But a funny thing happened recently. On the way to Sydney's Kingsford-Smith Airport, I stopped at a petrol station right under the flight path. A huge 747 was flying over, so low it looked as if it was about to clip the roof of the petrol station. When I went to pay for my petrol, I asked the guy on the cash register how he handled the noise. Guess what he said? 'What noise?'! I thought he was joking, but he was completely serious. Because he had worked there for ten years, he had subconsciously trained himself to screen out the aircraft noise – for sanity's sake. His last comment to me was, 'Mate, if I noticed every aircraft that went over, I would end up going mad!'

SUCCESS CAN BE SCREENED OUT

Sometimes putting on 'mind-blinkers' can be a bad thing. Just like you can screen out the noise of a 747 overhead, you can screen out success.

As I describe in Chapter 10, you attract in life whatever you think you are worthy of. So one of the first steps to 'getting lucky' in any area of your life is to decide that you *deserve* whatever it is you want, for example, a more satisfying job, a lover, more money etc. In other words, stop screening out success and start creating your own 'luck'.

When I share the information in this chapter in my seminar, I find that many people accept very quickly the idea that we *create* luck – that luck is not something that just happens. But I have also noticed that people can be very selective about luck. On one hand, they accept that they are attracting in their life all the good luck they deserve, but on the other, they are reluctant to accept that they are attracting bad luck for the same reason.

Rachel, a cosmetics salesperson for a large department store, came up to me during afternoon tea in a recent seminar. She said that I had hit the nail right on the head when I said that many of us are selective about the kind of luck we attract in our lives. She told me that over the past year she had let her level of self-esteem fall. She had broken up with her boyfriend of three years and then, two months later, her brother had died of cancer.

While everyone around her had been sympathetic, Rachel said what she had really needed after a few months was someone to give her a good talking-to and tell her to stop feeling sorry for herself. 'Everyone was too scared to say anything like that because they didn't want to hurt me further. But the truth is, if I hadn't come to this seminar today, I would most probably have gone on feeling sorry for myself for another twelve months'.

What have you been blocking out up to now that could have helped you to achieve more success?

HOW TO CREATE YOUR OWN 'LUCK'

This is one of the hardest decisions to make, but when you finally do it, you will never look back. The decision I am talking about is your commitment to take total accountability for what is happening in your life.

You can set all the goals you like, be as positive as you can and work as hard as the next person – but you will still achieve very little if you don't take total Locus of Control for your successes and failures. How much of what is happening in your world do you think *you* control and how much do you think is left to chance?

When I Win the Big One
With so much hype and media attention on gambling, it's really no wonder that Australians spend billions of dollars every year on trying to improve their lifestyle.

Let's get something straight first. I am not one of those people who wants to control what everyone does with their free time and hard-earned money. I believe that it's up to you what you do with them – after all, this chapter (and this whole book!) is about taking control of your life. But I want to make sure you know what you're doing when you put all your hopes and dreams into something that you can't control or manage, like gambling.

Dennis, a thirty-five-year-old stock controller who attended one of my seminars, is a case in point. He had worked for nearly twenty years (having left school in Year 10), and was still trying to make ends meet. He said that he was dumbfounded at my presentation because he felt as if I was talking about his life.

He said that, for as long as he could remember, he had always dreamt of taking one year off work and travelling around the world. But he said that he had always felt that if he didn't win a substantial amount of money from one of the lotteries, he couldn't go on his trip. Dennis said that after hearing me speak, he realised he had been caught up in the media hype and had given total Locus of Control to something he couldn't control – the lotteries and gambling.

How many people do you know who can't wait to race down to the newsagency to buy a scratch ticket or put in their entry for the weekly lottery draw? Locus of Control is basically how much accountability you are taking for your success in life – how much you think you control what happens in your world. Reading the stars, going to clairvoyants, addictive casino visits and obsessive lottery ticket purchases are all signs that you have given up hope on yourself – that you don't think you can do it!

Well, you can. But first, you have to make one big decision. From now on, your rewards and successes in life are going to come only from your own efforts. Your successes are going to come from being focused. Your goals and aspirations are going to be realised by your resilience and tenacity – by having a plan and sticking to it, no matter how difficult things get.

Impatience Implies Self-doubt

When you cut to the chase, gambling is all about self-doubt. It's about not loving yourself, and therefore trying to get the universe to give you something that you know in your heart you do not deserve. It's trying to get something for nothing, and as everyone knows, there's no such thing as a free lunch. There is nothing for nothing in this world. If you think you have received something for nothing, go back and have a good look. You may be surprised what you paid for it in other ways.

YOU ARE ALWAYS IN THE RIGHT PLACE AT THE RIGHT TIME

You're probably thinking, 'What a crazy heading!' But it's true. You have always been in the right place at the right time. When you clarify your thinking and really focus your mind on what you want, you will suddenly find yourself attracting events and people to your life to make your goals a reality.

There is only one way to prove that what I am saying will work for you, and that is to put it into action. The next chapter, 'Goal-setting', really demonstrates that without a clear destination – whether for tomorrow or for further into the future – you are like a ship in the ocean with no rudder and no captain, drifting endlessly, hoping that a strong wind will arrive and push you along.

If you are hoping for luck to come out of thin air, that is what you are doing – drifting. Don't let media hype or gambling advertising fool you. *You are creating your current level of luck.* And if you are not satisfied with that level, keep reading! Once you start to see where you want to go in life with a bit more focus, you'll wonder why you didn't start setting regular goals a lot earlier.

CHAPTER FOUR

Goal-setting: How to Get More Focus in Your Life

'Goals are dreams with deadlines.'
PAUL HANNA

IN THIS CHAPTER:

Why you must focus on what you want,
not on what you *don't* want

✳

How to see yourself successful using visualisation

✳

Preparing yourself for future success

✳

Why writing your goals down is a must

✳

The difference between millionaires and billionaires

✳

How clear and focused goals make you stronger

✳

Why a goal without a deadline will remain a dream

✳

How to save more money with goal-setting

✳

Why having no 'escape route' keeps you focused
on your goals

✳

Why feedback is essential to stay focused

W hen I was on a recent speaking tour of Australia for BMW, one of the salespeople, Mike, described how he had once attended an advanced driver-training seminar. One of the first exercises involved being at the wheel, and then suddenly applying the brakes on a skidpan (a wet surface which simulates braking in wet conditions). Strategically placed right in front of the driver was an oversized witch's hat, similar to the ones you see on the side of the road when repairs are being done. The idea was very simple: hit the brakes, turn the wheel, and miss the witch's hat. Mike said that, without exception, everyone hit it. And everyone had excuses.

DON'T FOCUS ON OBSTACLES

As the driving program progressed, the participants became acutely aware of one of the most fundamental lessons in skilled driving. What everyone did as they braked was notice the oversized witch's hat staring at them. And then, bingo – they moved towards whatever they looked at. By the end of the day's instruction, everyone was easily handling the car and missing the witch's hat.

So what changed? Mike explains: 'All the instructor did was ask every person to do the following: instead of looking at the witch's hat when they were skidding, they had to look at where they wanted to go. While it was difficult at first, everyone started to get the feel of it and then it became easy'.

Those drivers were given a concrete example of what happens when you are distracted by an obstacle. Life is pretty much the same. If you keep on thinking about and looking at what you *don't* want to happen, there is a pretty good chance that you will move towards it.

FantaSEE YOUR SUCCESS
(Visualise Your Goals)

I have created a new word to describe the process of visualising where you want to go: 'FantaSEE'. Sportspeople have no problem with this principle. They know it works. They use it.

In one of my partners' seminars, Kevin, who is a darts champion, said that when preparing for a championship, he goes to bed thinking only about the dartboard – and, in particular, the bull's-eye. As part of his mental rehearsal, he closes his eyes and imagines the bull's-eye – the end result – as big as the board itself. By visualising this constantly, over and over again, Kevin ends up reinforcing the picture of an oversized bull's-eye in his mind. He thinks all the time about the bull's-eye, not about letting go of the dart. And that's how he became a champion.

During a recent tournament in Australia, Greg Norman was asked whether his putting had let him down. Without hesitation, the Shark said it had nothing to do with his putting: 'I just haven't been seeing the ball fall into the hole as clearly as I usually do'. In other words, he wasn't focusing enough on the end result because he was spending too much time thinking about his swing.

If you don't focus on a very specific objective, chances are your potential will never really come to the surface. When was the last time you walked into McDonald's and asked, 'Can I have some food?' Sounds crazy, I know. The right way to order in Macca's is to arrive at the counter, make a selection from the menu board, pay for it, and then bon appetit! What's the difference with life?

> # Be specific in your order. (Focus)
> # Pay for it. (Hard work and
> # determination)
> # Enjoy. (The spoils)

YOUR IMAGINATION IS YOUR FLIGHT SIMULATOR

Have you ever flown into Hong Kong? If you haven't, ask someone who has what the landing was like. They will probably use words like 'scary', 'exciting' or 'unbelievable'. All these words are correct. On the final approach to Kai Tak Airport the plane circles steep mountains, like a shark circling its prey. To get to the runway, it has to fly between buildings. Not *above* them – *between* them!

Let's say that an international airline wants one of their pilots to commence flying the Hong Kong sector. What do you think would happen if the pilot had never been to Hong Kong? Would the airline say, 'Get a 747, fill it with 300 passengers and have a few practice shots till you get it right'? I don't think so. They would have the pilot practise inside a flight simulator, which would allow him or her to see the 'actual' approach to Hong Kong Airport: mountains, buildings, water, the lot.

Getting the pilot to watch other pilots perform the landing wouldn't be as effective, because the pilot wouldn't have the same level of emotional involvement. With the simulator, he or she is able to feel the vibrations and hear the engine tones, as well as having the visual picture. With practice, this will make the pilot very confident about landing in Hong Kong.

Preparing a pilot to land in Hong Kong is the same as preparing yourself for success in life. When you start to imagine yourself having the qualities of someone you admire, and imagine it again and again, you will move in that direction. Your goal might be to obtain a material possession, such as a new stereo. Or you might want to change the way you react in a given situation – for example, to be calm when someone is annoying you. If you want to add more power to your goal-setting, start to imagine the goal NOW, as if you were already there.

The Car of His Dreams

Sam, a sports-car buff, told me he desperately wanted to own the car of his dreams, but felt it was further away than ever. When I asked him what he had done to trigger his emotions and get focused on having the car, he said he didn't know what I meant. The only reminder he ever received was when he caught a fleeting glance of someone else driving the same style of car, or at the annual motor show.

After learning about the power of visualisation, Sam started to FantaSEE his new sports car. He went to a car dealer who specialised in this type of car and obtained three colour brochures. As soon as he got home, Sam cut out a large photo of his dream car and stuck it on the ceiling above his bed. Now the first thing he sees every morning and the last thing he sees every night is the photo.

As Sam focused more and more on his 'new car', he started to realise how much money he was wasting on doing things to his current car. He made a decision not to spend one more cent on it. From now on all his money would go towards saving for his new car.

Sam learnt in my seminar that what you focus on in life expands, so it came as no surprise for me to hear that when other temptations arose, such as going out with his mates for a boozy weekend, he found that he didn't just jump in and accept the invitation. Instead he began screening all the money he was spending and cutting the wastage. Before he had become really serious about owning his new car, he would buy anything and everything that came his way. Now he was comparing everything to his new car – and how do you think everything else rated? That's right. The car was now the focus.

Sam called to let me know that he was right on target in his savings plan and could not believe how much money he was saving now that he was focused on his goal.

> # You move in the direction of your dominant thoughts.

WRITE YOUR GOALS DOWN

In the USA, a survey was conducted to try and find out the major difference, if any, between millionaires and billionaires. I was intrigued by the outcome, which found that while there were many differences between the individuals surveyed, the only true difference between millionaires and billionaires was that millionaires read their goals once a day and billionaires read theirs twice a day. It was as simple as that!

How many times today have you read *your* goals? How many times this week have you read your goals? Have you read your goals this year? Wait a minute – have you written them down?

When I first started speaking, I heard a saying that the majority of people will die having achieved only about 3 per cent of their potential. How can you possibly reach your potential if you have not taken the time to think about what you want and then committed your goals to paper?

One of the most common questions I am asked is, 'Why do I have to write my goals down?' The answer surprises many people: when you write down your goals, you are convincing yourself that you can achieve them. Remember, the world is your mirror, so before you start trying to convince the world of something, you must first ensure that you are certain *you* believe in what you are striving for.

When I bump into people on the street or in shopping centres who have been to my seminars, they often tell me what's happened in their life. Many times, as they are speaking to me, they hear themselves say what they have achieved, and then realise that they set out to achieve a certain goal, and actually did achieve it.

Everyone is in the same boat. We are all moving very fast, with more demands on our time than ever before. If you are going to achieve your potential, one of the first and most important steps is to clarify what you want. Writing down your goals brings what you want into sharp focus and maintains the momentum in your life.

Try it yourself. Write a goal no more than one line in length, and place it on the vanity mirror in your bathroom so when you shave or put on your make-up, you are constantly reminded about who you want to become or where you want to be.

About five years ago I was conducting a seminar for twenty-five millionaire car dealers. They were all doing extremely well in their business and all testified to the power of keeping your goals in front of you as much as you can. When I asked them how they did this, one dealer said he writes his personal goals on a small card and places it in his shaving cabinet so that he glances at them every morning. Another said that he and his wife put their goals on the back of the toilet door in their ensuite – they are the only people reading them and he reckoned they would see them at least twice a day! There were many other responses: on the back of the mobile phone, in the wallet, on the dashboard of the car, and so on.

The most diligent and determined method of keeping your goals in front of you was told to me by a leading salesperson in the finance industry. Gail is very successful and well respected by her peers. She said that she records herself reading her goals out loud onto a tape using her answering machine. On her way to work, and driving between appointments, Gail plays her tape over and over again, convincing herself what sort of person she wants to become.

It's emotive, private and in her own words. Sold!

PUT SETBACKS INTO PERSPECTIVE BY READING YOUR GOALS AGAIN

Whenever a setback occurs after you have set a goal for yourself, one of the major spin-offs is that you will compare the setback to the goal.

Here's an example. Think about how you feel when you're getting ready to go on leave. Months before, you find yourself thinking about the holiday and how good it's going to be. As departure day gets closer you start to think about it more often. What happens if there is a setback at work on Wednesday, and your departure day is Saturday? How do you react? Most people would take it in their stride, look at the calendar and exclaim: 'Three days to go!'

But what would happen if there was no holiday and you had this setback? It's hard to tell, but I believe the majority of people would get upset, and the setback might play on their thinking for at least a couple of days.

It's not what upsets you, but how long you stay upset for. Successful people know that they are just as likely to have their fair share of setbacks. Goals don't stop setbacks from happening, they just put them into perspective. So when you have a setback, read your goals again!

OBJECTIONS ARE PARAMOUNT TO YOUR SUCCESS

'Objections are a request for more information.' Every salesperson who has achieved success in their chosen field knows this statement to be true. They know that when you come to buy something from them, you come with a list of objections, or questions, that when solved, result in the sale happening. When you have a clear and focused target or goal, you are more likely to persist through any objections, because you know that when you do, you will be closer to your goal. Why would you persist if you didn't know what you wanted? For many of us, that's what happens during everyday life. We have setbacks, and we fight them instead of accepting them as getting us closer to our goals.

I remember vividly when I first started my business, and the pain of knockback after knockback, rejection after rejection. My self-esteem took a battering and I wondered on many occasions whether it was all worth it. And just as quickly as the question popped into my head, my self-talk crushed it with the answer: 'You wanted to work for yourself, you're the one who wants the great cars and trips, you're the one who said you would never work for anyone again. Shut up and get back to work'.

My biggest lesson in persistence came when I visited Sean, one of my current clients, for the first time. I had tried unsuccessfully to get his business.

I wanted to put all his people through my seminar, but he was sceptical. He kept on giving great excuses (objections) as to why he could not afford me; his organisation did not need any motivation. On my sixth visit to Sean, he suddenly became very positive towards me. Gone were the excuses on why he could not use me – they were replaced by reasons why he should give me a go. We eventually agreed to conduct a pilot seminar with twenty of his staff to see if they thought it would benefit the company.

Two weeks after the pilot seminar, I received a commitment to put every person in Sean's organisation through my seminar. Last year, nearly five years to the day that we held the first seminars in his organisation, Sean and I were having lunch. Out of the blue he said to me: 'Do you realise that you came back to see me six times, and it was on the sixth visit that I agreed to purchase the pilot seminar?'

I started laughing and acknowledged his recollection. Then he hit me with a king hit! Well, a big lesson anyway. He said he never gives anyone business until he is convinced they really want to work with his organisation. He told me that most salespeople knock on his door, get one no, or maybe two nos, and then are never seen again. 'When I know someone comes back on the sixth visit, I know they really want my business'.

SET A DEADLINE

You're kidding yourself if you don't put a deadline on your dreams. Because without a deadline, that's what they will remain: dreams.

Let's have a look at what happens when you put a deadline on a dream. Say you have always wanted to visit Australia's fantastic Great Barrier Reef. You have read about it since you were seven, and now it's time to see it in person. All the visualisation techniques and colour brochures will be a waste of time if you don't commit with a deadline departure date.

One of the first lessons we learnt in goal-setting was that when we are clearly focused, we start to see how to achieve our goals. As soon as you decide that you are departing on a Qantas flight at 2.30 pm on Saturday afternoon, 26 August, guess what happens? From now on, everything and anything to do with the Great Barrier Reef will start to show itself to you.

The goal comes first and then you see how to achieve it.

In my seminar, I ask everyone to imagine they have a brother living on the beach at Scarborough, Western Australia. He has been at them to visit for years, but they always fob him off with 'One day I'll get there'.

In the next break at the seminar, I ask everyone to imagine that a phone call comes through. It's your sister-in-law from Perth, ringing to tell you that your brother has just been involved in a head-on collision and the doctors think he might not make it through the night. I ask everyone, 'Who knows Qantas or Ansett's reservation numbers?' Typically, no one can remember the reservation numbers because in their day-to-day working environment, they have no need to know them. The only exception I find is if someone in the seminar has a job that requires constant dealing with airlines. In such jobs, these numbers are essential information.

But let's have a look at what happens when you know you have to get to Perth immediately. Suddenly, the reservation numbers become essential information. What happens next? You ring Directory Assistance to get the numbers, then you ring the airlines to find out their schedules and prices. Then you . . . Can you see now what happens when you decide to put a deadline on a goal? Everything you need to get to the goal suddenly becomes essential information, and you allow it to come into your awareness.

BE SPECIFIC

One of the first questions I ask in my seminar is 'Who is always running out of money?' And nearly every hand goes up. Some people put up two hands!

Lorraine, a senior manager for a pharmaceutical company, said that while she had no problems earning a good income, she did have problems hanging on to her money. She said that it seemed to go as quickly as she earned it.

My question is this: why would you want to save your money if you didn't have a good reason to do so? In other words, goals not only give us perspective when we have setbacks, they also ensure that we gain perspective when we spend our hard-earned income. Let's say you want to buy yourself a new camera. You're sick and tired of getting photos back that are sub-standard because of your old, cheap camera. You're serious now. You know the features you want, the brand and how much you can afford. You know you want it by Christmas, and you're determined . . .

We are all tempted to buy impulsively, on the spot. What do you think happens when your new camera is only one month away, and you see a stylish outfit in that boutique in the city? This is the key to keeping your money. Goal-setters know that they get tempted just like everyone else, but what keeps them from actually buying the unwanted impulsive gift for themselves is – you guessed it – goals.

Nick, an apprentice, said he didn't really notice how much time and money he was spending going out with his mates nearly every night of the week. Yet he wondered why, after three years of work, he still had nothing to show for his efforts. Two apprentices in his class were raving about the great time they just had in Bali, surfing at Uluwatu and Granjagan (G Land), two of Indonesia's most popular surfing locations. They were the same age as Nick, and had started work on virtually the same day. Nick said he realised that he had never bothered to save his money, because he thought Bali was out of reach. But now, having seen these two suntanned mates, he was convinced he could do it.

When I followed up with Nick, he said the most remarkable thing to happen was that he had started to look forward more to Bali than to going out each night. While he hasn't become a hermit, he has toned down the social life, and started to get a bit more focus. His saving pattern has increased unbelievably and he has noticed his self-esteem improving – he now feels a great sense of achievement, and he hasn't even left Australia!

COMMITMENT – FAILURE IS NOT AN OPTION

In order to meet your goals, you must have commitment. This concept is hard to put into words, so I will use a 2000-year-old Chinese story from *The Art of War* by Sun Tzu to explain it.

In his book, Sun Tzu shares the tale of a troop leader and his troops preparing to invade an island. They arrive on the island in ten small boats, ready and prepared to take on the enemy. To get to the township on the island, they have to climb a small hill. Just before they reach the top of the hill and start their onslaught, the troop leader tells his men to turn around and look at the boats they have just arrived on. To their horror, the boats are on fire. The troop leader has burnt and sunk their only means of escape.

How do you think these men will now go into the attack? How much more resilient will they be when suffering casualties? How much more determined do you think they will be, whichever way the attack goes?

If you are serious about commitment, either in a relationship, your career, or, for that matter, anything, you must decide to burn the escape boats in your life, because when they are available you will use them, usually at the first sign of trouble.

I will never forget the response I received from an elderly woman, Rose, in one of my seminars in Adelaide. I had just finished talking about the above example when she suddenly said, 'Young man, you're spot on!' When I asked her what she meant, she said, 'That's the problem today with most marriages and relationships. They are not prepared to commit to each other'. She said that in most marriage ceremonies, the line 'For better, for worse, for richer, for poorer' means 'For richer, or forget it'.

Rose went on to say that most couples of her generation had been through extremely tough times, especially during the Second World War, but what kept them together was their commitment to each other. As they saw it, they had no escape route. She said that when the escape route is burnt on your relationship, no matter what happens you will make it work.

GET PROGRESS REPORTS TO STAY ON TARGET

One of the most intriguing things when you are driving anywhere is the amount of information you are expected to take in – 'Pedestrians ahead', 'Stop', 'Homebush Bay 15 km', 'Give way', 'Roundabout ahead' . . . the list goes on. Can you remember when you drove from one major city in your state to another, such as Brisbane to the Gold Coast or Sydney to Newcastle? How many signs did you read to get to your destination? Hundreds, I bet. And each one assisted you in getting to your goal.

Can you imagine how confusing it would have been if there were no signs? Well, there's not much difference between driving to a destination, and setting a goal and striving to reach it. In both instances, plenty of progress reports are required. Without these, you might take ages to arrive, or worse still, you might not arrive at all.

Ken Blanchard and Spencer Johnson, co-authors of the best-seller *The One Minute Manager*, said: 'Feedback is the breakfast of champions'. We need progress reports, or feedback, to keep on the right path, because it's so easy to lose our way or get out of control. Take speed-limit signs. They change constantly, and we have two choices. We can take note and adjust our speed to match the new limit, or we can keep speeding, not take notice of the feedback (that is, the sign), and cop the speeding ticket which will eventually be handed to us.

Have you ever wondered how heat-seeking missiles hit their target with unswerving accuracy? They have their clear and focused goal: the target. Then when the missile is fired, it self-talks, asking 'How am I doing in relationship to where I want to be, that is, the target?' The mechanism on board is constantly saying 'Higher, higher, lower, lower', and adjusts accordingly. This happens again and again, every split second, until, whammo! It hits its target.

GOALS ARE YOUR JIGSAW BOXTOP

Have you ever attempted to do a jigsaw puzzle without the boxtop as a guide? If you were ever asked to, you'd probably look around for the 'Just Kidding' camera crew and expect to hear any moment that they were having you on.

Why is it, then, that we try to put our lives together without a 'boxtop'? Goals are your boxtop to life. They keep you focused and looking forward. Most importantly, they allow you to put the pieces together a lot more easily than if you tried to do so without any sort of guide.

And here's some great news. If you have managed to reach where you are now with no real focused plans and goals, just imagine what's in store for you down the track once you decide to become more focused!

CHAPTER FIVE

I've Had It – Enough's Enough!

'The lowest ebb is the turn of the tide.'

ANONYMOUS

IN THIS CHAPTER:

When you want something badly enough, you will change

✳

The drive of a lifetime in a 240K GL

✳

How a public humiliation changed a person's life

✳

How a woman broke free from an abusive relationship

✳

The last smoke – 'That's it, I've finished'

✳

How low do you have to fall?

W ithout exception, every successful person I know has shared with me an event which happened on their journey that gave them a big shake-up or caused them to say 'Enough's enough' – an event in their life that made them decide that they deserved to be flying at a higher altitude and that they weren't going to stay at the lower altitude any longer.

As much as I want to help you improve your life in the area you want to, you must understand that your *commitment to change* is the first and most important step. You've read about self-esteem and goal-setting, and learnt that we all have an awesome power inside of us. But what determines whether you *use* this power? It's the decision not to accept the current state of events any more.

WHEN WILL I KNOW I'VE HAD ENOUGH?

How do you know when you can't take any more? When you are *really* ready to break out of the current mould created by your old beliefs.

A story I heard in New York about ten years ago will show you what I mean. I was waiting for a train in the notorious subway when I saw a busker, aged about forty-five, saying 'Repent, repent' and telling stories while people waited for their subway train to arrive. Well, I, like everyone near me, was laughing at him when, before I knew it, I found myself paying attention to him.

What drew my attention was this story. A man, disillusioned with where his life was going, went to a master of an ancient Eastern religion and asked,

'When will I know what true enlightenment is? When will I know why we are all here on this planet?' The two men were standing next to a pond. The master reached out and put his hand on the man's head, and started to push downwards. Then he started to push him under the water.

The man did not fight, because he thought the master had something mysterious in store for him. After about fifteen seconds under the water, the man realised the master was not going to let him up for air, so he started to resist a little. Then, after this had no effect, he decided to get serious and push the master out of the way.

The master still wouldn't let up, so the man lunged furiously upward and pushed the master away, taking a frantic gasp for air. 'Why did you do that, Master? You could have killed me!' said the man, confused.

The master responded: 'When you desire enlightenment as much as you just desired air, then you will see the way'.

The Drive in the 240K GL

My 'gasping for air' came about two years into my business. It wasn't going well, and the bills were mounting up. Clients were rejecting me one after another, and I thought to myself, 'Is this really worth the pain I'm going through?'

To raise enough funds to keep going, I decided that, as much as I loved my car, it would have to go. It was painful attending the auction and watching someone snap up a bargain midnight-blue BMW, but I was determined that my business would survive. I was not going to quit. For the next eighteen months, I had no car, and travelled to appointments and events on public transport or walked there.

One Saturday I was invited to a cousin's wedding. I caught a train out to the western suburbs where the wedding was being held, feeling shocking. I had started to develop a sore throat, and the 30-degree temperature on the train had not helped. After the wedding, Sue, my sister-in-law, seeing how much pain I was in, offered to lend me her trusty Datsun 24OK GL for the drive home. I was thankful, because the last thing I wanted to do was ride back on the train.

The drive home in the 24OK GL was a life-changing experience for me. It wasn't that anything major happened on the way; it's just that as I was driving home, my thoughts were very focused. As thankful as I was for the car, I made a decision there and then that enough was enough. I was going to stop feeling sorry for myself and get on with it.

From that moment on, my business started to fire. It didn't happen overnight, but I could see that for the first time in my life I was without a car, and I hated it. I had reached what for me was the lowest point, and now I could start to climb back.

The Flight of Her Life

Carol, an energetic secretary in her early forties, came up to me at the end of one of my Brisbane seminars and said she had related to everything I said about 'Enough's enough'. She told me about *her* 'gasping for air'.

She had been on her annual Christmas flight to Sydney to see the in-laws when the moment struck. Her husband, Barry, a labourer, knew Carol found flying uncomfortable because of her weight, and had suggested that this year they could pay the extra and fly business class. But Carol knew they couldn't afford it and said no. 'It's only an hour', she recalled saying.

But it turned out to be literally the flight of her life. Doctors had told her that if she didn't lose some weight she would die a young woman, but Carol said that the doctors' advice didn't have as much impact as squeezing into her economy seat that time. She was very embarrassed and, to make matters worse, could not lock her seat belt. The turning point came when the flight attendant handed Carol a 'special' seat belt and said, 'Try this, ma'am. You might have better luck'. Carol was furious (as was Barry), but the attendant's comment had a huge impact. Carol decided right then to lose weight now. Not next month, but NOW.

Carol said this was the moment she said, 'I've had it – enough's enough'. Over the next few months, she lost twenty kilos. The woman I met at my seminar was happy and healthy – because she had taken control of her life.

I Won't Take It Any More

Joan, a woman in her fifties, shared her amazing story with me at the end of one of my corporate seminars. At the time I met her, she was working to 'get back on her feet' after escaping from an abusive marriage of more than twenty-five years.

Joan said that when we started to discuss 'Enough's enough' in the seminar, she went into a sort of trance. She started to look at her life and how the abuse had started slowly and then got worse over time. Joan said that when she looked back now, she could see that she should have got out of the relationship. When she told me why she had stayed, she hit the nail right on the head: 'I didn't think I could survive without him.'

She went on: 'I was so lacking in self-esteem and had such a poor self-image that I thought my only choice was to accept what was happening'. She had finally realised she needed assistance when her partner lost his job and became so bitter that his abuse became intolerable. Joan said that she weighed up all her options and it became abundantly clear that she had nothing to lose if she left. Nothing could be as bad as what she was putting up with at that moment.

Joan said that it was now nearly two years since she had left her partner, and that it has been a struggle. In hindsight, she realised she was in the driver's seat of her life and could have left her partner at any time.

For me, the most telling feature of Joan's story is that she really made it clear why people stay in bad relationships and put up with so much rubbish. She said that if she had known about self-image and goal-setting earlier, there is no way she would have stayed. But twenty years ago there were very few support groups and self-development seminars.

Joan's story clearly explains how, when you let your self-esteem and opinion of yourself fall, you will let the most devastating things happen to you, and feel powerless to stop them.

This Is the Last Smoke

One of my clients, Eric, said that his literal 'gasping for air' was at exactly 10.45 am on a balmy October day five years ago, when he was on holiday.

He was visiting Stanley Chasm and decided that he would join his travelling companions in exploring this fabulous site a bit further. There were huge boulders to climb and Eric soon dropped behind. He couldn't believe it. Here he was, fit, or so he thought, and his friends, some of whom were overweight, were way ahead of him. At the time, Eric was a moderately heavy smoker. He said that he had tried everything to give up smoking, but nothing had worked until he ran out of breath that day at Stanley Chasm.

72

On his return home, Eric didn't give up cold turkey, but he did make a commitment to reduce his intake by a certain amount each day. This way, just like when he had started on one or two smokes a day and had gradually increased, his habit of reducing would continue until he gave up completely.

HOW LOW DO YOU HAVE TO FALL?

We are all different, and how we react to stress and setbacks varies. Successful people have a level of self-esteem that allows them to recognise how they should be treated. They know when someone is treating them with less respect than they know they deserve, and they make decisions very quickly to remove themselves from this negative environment.

How long will you put up with your friends making negative comments to you or about you before you take action? How long before *you* decide 'Enough's enough'?

Call them 'moments of truth' or 'rites of passage' – these events propel us to making a commitment to change and to moving forward in a different direction to improve our lives. They might be painful at the time, and could be your 'lowest ebb', but don't discount the power of what happens in your mind when you decide 'Enough's enough'!

CHAPTER SIX

SuccessSpeak©

'Success doesn't come the way
you think it does, it comes from
the way you think.'

ROBERT SCHULLER

IN THIS CHAPTER:

How to attract success using SuccessSpeak

✳

The SuccessSpeak challenge

✳

How SuccessSpeak affirmations can literally
change how you feel

✳

From Self-esteem Zapping to SuccessSpeak

✳

Talk yourself up to success

T hink of someone you know who is very successful in their chosen career. How do they speak? Which words do they use to describe how they feel about themselves and life in general? When you ask how they are going, do they say 'Oh, all right' or do they return with a big 'Fantastic!', 'Excellent!', 'Powering!'? You can bet they'll be using positive, upbeat words to describe their situation.

You see, words trigger pictures in your mind, which then trigger emotions, which in turn decide how you feel on a given day. Which words do you find yourself using often? While 'self-talk' is the things you say or think to yourself, I have created two terms to describe the things you say out loud: 'SuccessSpeak' for the positive ones, and 'Self-esteem Zapping Statements' for the negative ones.

This is a very important issue – how you talk about things really does have a huge impact on how you feel. Take the weather, for example. How do you describe the weather when you are discussing it with a taxi driver? If it's raining you might use a Self-esteem Zapping Statement such as, 'I hate rainy days', or if it's a stinking-hot summer afternoon you might similarly whinge and complain. Another way to look at this sort of weather is to appreciate Australia's climatic variations, and the freedom you have to experience them. Turn your weather observations into SuccessSpeak, and see how different you feel about life in general!

THE SuccessSpeak CHALLENGE

It takes twenty-one days to break (or form) a habit, good or bad. I'm challenging you to break your habit of using Self-esteem Zapping Statements and replace them with SuccessSpeak.

The following list should assist you in finding where you sit on the SuccessSpeak challenge. What would you reply to the following questions?

How's work?
Hi, how are you going?
What's happening?
Did you have a good weekend?
How's the family?

This is just a simple test, but you can quickly see if you habitually use SuccessSpeak or talk your way down into the dumps.

For the next three weeks, see if you can be conscious of the words you use. You'll be amazed at the negative statements that come out of your mouth. Many of these will have been picked up unconsciously, at work or at home – but it doesn't matter where they came from. Write them down before you go to bed at night. After a few days, if you start to see a pattern, try to stop yourself using these statements in conversations from now on. Break the habit and see how much better you start to feel.

SuccessSpeak AFFIRMATIONS

An 'affirmation' is something that, when said often enough, becomes real.

This is certainly not a new idea. Most religions believe in the power of affirmations but call them by other names, such as prayers, chants, petitions etc. If you want to change the way you feel about your job, relationship or life in general, try using SuccessSpeak affirmations. As I said before, it takes twenty-one days to change a belief or habit, so get started now and watch how your moods start to become more consistent and your general outlook on life begins to lift.

SuccessSpeak©

On the left side of the chart below, you will see everyday statements which zap your self-esteem every time you say them. Change them into the SuccessSpeak affirmations on the right, and watch the dramatic effect they have on how you feel and act towards yourself and, of course, your friends and family. Like goals, affirmations should be written down and read at least once a day, every day. Remember the 'millionaires and billionaires' story? The more you keep your goals in front of you, the more you move in that direction.

Self-esteem Zapping Statements	SuccessSpeak Affirmations
I'm having a shocker of a day.	My day is improving.
I am at my wits' end.	I am in the pilot's seat of my life.
I hate my job. It's boring.	Every day I like my job more.
I can't stand my boss.	My boss respects and trusts me.
I'll never get ahead here. It's not what you know, but who you know.	I am in control of my job. I will be promoted when I am ready.
Our relationship has hit a brick wall. It's going nowhere.	Our love for each other grows every day.
I have a lousy temper, just like my old man.	I am always calm and relaxed. Nothing fazes me.
I am always late. I just can't get it right.	I am on time every time.
Everyone's out to get me.	Everyone is very relaxed with me.
You can't trust anyone.	People trust me because I trust me.
I'm depressed.	I'm pumping.
Life's a pain.	Life's fantastic.
Kids don't respect adults these days. Not like when I was a kid.	I relate to all my kids. They trust me and see me as their best friend.
Screw the competition.	There's enough for all of us.

TALK YOURSELF UP TO SUCCESS

In nearly every seminar I ask the question, 'How many of you think right now that you deserve better than you have?' In most cases, about 98 per cent of people put up their hand, signalling that they want to improve. So I know for sure just via this very informal research that most people want to improve. Yet when I ask how many of them think that the way they *speak* could be holding them back, most leave their hands firmly in their laps until we get to the SuccessSpeak part of the seminar.

Ted was an unemployed former public servant when I met him at a seminar at his partner's company. He said that he had been watching an old home video of his brother's wedding about a week earlier, and was struck by the positive, happy-go-lucky spirit he, Ted, had displayed in the video. Everyone had been laughing and having a good time, but he was at the centre of the action.

He realised how far he had let himself slip since he was made redundant fifteen months earlier. He said that his general demeanour had become downbeat, and that after listening to me he could now see that the words he was using every day were maintaining his low self-image and lack of confidence. No matter what his partner, Sue, said, he had not been able to see how down he was until he watched the wedding video. It was the king hit he needed to make him lift his game. Sue had suggested that he come along to the seminar – other people's partners were attending and she thought he might get a few pointers to lift him out of the hole he was in.

About two months after the seminar, Ted landed a job in the local newsagency – exactly the job he had always said he would do when he 'won the lottery'. While he didn't own the newsagency, he was managing it and was now 'living' his dream instead of waiting for it to land in his lap. Sue told me that she has never seen him so motivated, and that once he has made this job work, he plans to buy his own newsagency and is confident it will be a success.

IT CREEPS UP ON YOU

Can you remember the last time you caught a cold? You probably started to feel a little 'off' at first, then you got a bit 'nasally', then the cramps and headaches came, and before you knew it, you were in the medical-centre lobby waiting to see your GP.

SuccessSpeak works in the same gradual way (but it makes you feel better, not worse!). If you keep reaffirming good opinions of yourself as part of your daily schedule, you will start to see a slow shift in your attitude to a more positive and upbeat style. The opposite also applies: if you lose your focus on SuccessSpeak and let yourself drift to Self-esteem Zapping Statements, before you know it you will be down in the dumps, blaming the world for everything.

Take the time right now to formulate some simple SuccessSpeak statements reaffirming that YOU CAN DO IT.

WANT TO KNOW MORE ABOUT . . . ?

Turn to . . .

CHAPTER SEVEN

Enthusiasm and Success

'The only thing more catching
than enthusiasm ... is lack
of enthusiasm.'

ANONYMOUS

IN THIS CHAPTER:

What does 'enthusiasm' mean?

✳

How your eyes are the window to your soul

✳

How emotion follows motion

✳

Why how you carry yourself determines how you feel

✳

How your enthusiasm encourages those around you

✳

Why enthusiasm is the lubricant of life

T he English word 'enthusiasm' comes from a Greek word, 'entheo', which means 'the inspiration within us'. In other words, enthusiasm comes from within the soul of a person. You cannot maintain a level of enthusiasm if you are not happy about the way you are living your life. You could fake your enthusiasm, but eventually everyone would see through you. It would be obvious, because your soul would give it away.

> ## Your eyes are the window
> ## to your soul.

How you feel, and how you tell the world you are feeling, is communicated via your eyes. It is very hard for most people to tell a lie while looking someone straight in the eye, because in a sense they will see their true reflection, and nobody wants to see a dishonest self.

WHY SUNGLASSES MUST BE USED WISELY

A client of mine, Bob, told me this story. Janet, one of his salespeople, was struggling to achieve her sales target. She asked Bob to come on-site with her one day so he could give her a few pointers. On returning to the office,

Janet asked Bob where he thought she could improve. His reply went to the heart of this young salesperson's problem.

'Your clients don't trust you,' said Bob. Janet was flabbergasted and asked why. He answered, 'They can't see your eyes because you wear your sunglasses all the time'. Now the job Janet was doing required a lot of outside on-site work, which meant that she wanted to wear her sunglasses when it was very bright as she was concerned about the damage the sun might cause.

Bob agreed, but said, 'If you don't make eye contact, no one is going to give you the go-ahead for a project as large as the one you are working on. What's worse, when you went into the site office, you left your sunglasses on, which created more distrust. They would have thought, "There's no sun in here. What's she trying to hide?"'

Because Janet wore prescription glasses, she had felt it would be too inconvenient to carry two pairs of glasses with her, and that's why she had worn her sunglasses into the office. But after having this discussion, she realised how powerful the eyes really are and made sure she never wore the sunglasses inside again. Once she had grasped this, she found her performance improved dramatically.

EMOTION FOLLOWS MOTION

Did you read that heading right? Emotion follows motion. We have all heard the saying 'Which comes first – the chicken or the egg?' Well, luck is similar, in that you first have to *act* lucky (motion) before you *feel* lucky (emotion).

Many of us are waiting for that 'special day' which will change our luck and give our level of enthusiasm a lift – it might be the day you land that job you've always wanted, or, as discussed in Chapter 3, the day you win the lottery. And you'll most probably go on waiting. But there's a better way to kick-start your enthusiasm: when you start to act like you feel great, that you are 'on top of the world', your life will start to mirror the way you're acting.

When you start to walk faster, with a jump in your step, things start to improve. For one thing, people around you will start to see you differently. Remember the last time you arrived at work down in the dumps? Everyone who came in contact with you had no idea what the problem was – they just knew something was wrong. What happens when you come in a second time feeling down? Everyone starts to think, 'Hey, what's going on with her?' And if you come in a third time depressed, that's how people will treat you from now on. The crazy thing is, you have in fact *asked* them to treat you this way by your previous moods.

But the reverse also works. When you start to talk up how you feel, everyone starts to comment how things must be going well for you. Try speeding up your walk over the next week and watch what happens. You will automatically start to feel better for it, and it will show.

The Buck Stops Here

Jeremy was a very successful mobile-phone salesperson. He had been in his current job for more than five years and knew it well. But things were just not happening. As sales manager, he was being paid to get the most out of his young team, yet when I met him he was complaining how they were dropping the ball, and not getting enough sales in a market that was literally booming.

I asked Jeremy how he thought his team saw him at the moment. His reply summed up everything: 'Oh, I guess they think I'm a grumpy old sod'. His guys thought he had given up, so they, unconsciously, were trying less and less. In fact, Jeremy said he had been walking past the kitchen at work the other day and overheard one of the guys say to another, 'With the way he's going, we'll all be lucky to have a job by the end of the month'.

In Chapter 1, you discovered how your attitude controls your altitude in life. For Jeremy, this meant having a good hard look at why his guys had suddenly lost the plot. He knew that a lack of leadership and no enthusiasm would zap the best sales team, let alone one in a super-competitive market like mobile phones. He realised only the tough were going to survive, and that he needed to change his attitude – and fast.

Jeremy rang me two days after his consultation. He said he was amazed at how quickly his guys had picked up the vibes that he was back on track. They were unaware that he had met with me, but they knew that whatever had happened, it was now 'business as usual'. In fact, one of his best salespeople, who was leading the team every month, said that he had been just about to pull the plug and resign because he thought Jeremy had lost it.

Within a week, sales were pumping and, while they were not at record levels, Jeremy could see that his newfound enthusiasm was as catching as his lack of enthusiasm.

THE PHYSIOLOGICAL CONNECTION TO ENTHUSIASM

On a piece of paper, write down five mannerisms you use or habits you get into when you are depressed. You might fold your arms a lot, or let your standard of dress slip, or walk around with your head down. Now write down five mannerisms or habits you use when you are on top of the world, such as walking with a spring in your step, complimenting people or smiling more.

Writing down these lists has probably made it obvious to you that your emotions are connected to how you act physically, so a powerful way to increase your level of enthusiasm is to be more aware of the connection between motion and emotion. Once you're aware, you're 70 per cent there.

❋ ❋ ❋

I have always found myself attracted to enthusiastic people – the kind of people who are excited to be alive and always looking forward. Every time I am around someone enthusiastic, whether I am having a great day or a lousy day, I always end up feeling energised.

In the following poem, Henry Ford really hits the mark when it comes to enthusiasm. He didn't have much patience with people who were always complaining about their problems, but he was very generous to those who came to him with solutions.

Enthusiasm

You can do anything if you have enthusiasm.
Enthusiasm is the yeast that makes your hopes rise
to the stars.

Enthusiasm is the sparkle in your eyes,
the swing in your gait,
the grip of your hand,
the irresistible surge of will and
energy to execute your ideas.

Enthusiasts are fighters.
They have fortitude.
They have staying qualities.

Enthusiasm is at the bottom of all progress.
With it, there is accomplishment.
Without it there are only alibis.

Henry Ford

WANT TO KNOW MORE ABOUT . . . ?	Turn to . . .
How you create your own luck	Chapter 3
Self-esteem and enthusiasm	Chapter 2
Why failure is not an option	Chapter 4
Motivating others	Chapter 12

CHAPTER EIGHT

Turning Setbacks into Success

'Many of life's failures are people who did not realise how close they were to success when they gave up.'

THOMAS EDISON

IN THIS CHAPTER:

The Ken Tagg story – from poverty to
eight McDonald's stores

✻

Fear – from one comfort zone to the next

✻

How to pick yourself up when you're down

✻

How to visit a beach or a forest in your own
lounge room

✻

Why meditation is not just for Indian gurus

✻

Mix with positive people and you'll
end up like them

✻

When things are at their worst, don't quit

Do you know anyone successful? Have you had a chance to ask them how hard it was during the early years, when they were setting up their business or starting out in their quest for a sporting medal? If you do get the opportunity, I can just about guarantee that the person will give you a long list of setbacks they overcame during their quest for success. You see, setbacks are fundamental to achieving success. They are what make us take a good look at ourselves and decide if we really want what we say we want.

Every setback will be replaced with an equal or better opportunity if you stay focused on your goals. When you are firmly looking forward towards these goals, you compare your setbacks to them, and then decide how much you are going to let the setbacks upset or derail you.

People with no goals to focus on are pushed around like a ship without a rudder in a stormy sea. Imagine how frustrating it would be seeing all that blue water but not knowing where to go. Have you ever seen a round-the-world yachtie interviewed while at sea? All alone, these people overcome tremendous hardships to ensure that they achieve their goal of sailing around the world. It's the same with goals in your life.

THE KEN TAGG STORY

I am fortunate to meet some amazing people in my travels, but nothing prepared me for the dynamo called Ken Tagg. Ken is the largest McDonald's licensee in Australia, with eight stores in the Macarthur area of Sydney's western suburbs.

This is the story of how Ken went from a life of extreme poverty to being the employer of over 800 Australians, and it can only be described as truly inspirational. It lets all of us know that, no matter where we come from, no matter how poor or disadvantaged, we can still rise to the top of our chosen career if we remain determined and focused.

Ken says that there were three major turning points in his life which led him to where he is today. The first occurred when he was fourteen years old, living in a housing-commission house in Concord, in Sydney's inner western suburbs. His mother was blind and his father was a milkman.

The family was very poor, surviving only from week to week on his father's small wage. One day when Ken came home from school, his father had left. The family was in deep trouble, and it was decided that, if they were to stay together, Ken would have to leave school and become the breadwinner. He got a job at the Sydney Markets from Monday to Friday, and pumped petrol on weekends at a local service station. It was a struggle, but the family stayed together.

The second turning point came when Ken was eighteen, and he joined Coca-Cola as a truck driver. He stayed for twenty-two years, working his way up to a managerial position where he was responsible for introducing post-mix to Australia, New Zealand and the Pacific region. During this time, he embarked on sixteen years of night school to improve his education. All his free time went into doing assignments and research for his classes, all at his own expense. The competition was fierce within the Coca-Cola company, but Ken was determined to outperform the university graduates who were his peers. And he did.

The third turning point was when, like many other Australians, Ken decided he wanted to be his own boss. Nearing the magic age of forty, he did a stocktake of his life and decided that, while there were great years behind him, the best were yet to come.

McDonald's Australia was looking for local operators to share in the company's expansion to this region and Ken knew that this was his time. He knew that McDonald's was a hit in the USA and would be a hit in Australia. He knew he wanted to be a franchisee but he also knew that the task wouldn't be easy. He cashed in everything he had to set up his business, which was seen in the late 1970s as 'high risk'. He was approved on

13 December 1982, when his Minto store opened its doors for the first time. But it was tough going. For the first seven years, he lost money. For the first three years, Ken lived in a caravan just to keep the business afloat.

Today, his restaurants in the Campbelltown area have sales in excess of $20 million. He was named Australian Franchisee of the Year in 1994 and later that year was awarded the prestigious McDonald's Golden Arches Award in Las Vegas. And yet, when I first met him at his store in Campbelltown, I was taken aback at the modest way in which he runs his life.

From a kid living in poverty to a multimillionaire, Ken Tagg is proof that you can make it in any career, at any age, providing you take 100 per cent accountability for yourself. He is proof that setbacks are essential in shaping success and demonstrates, above all, that you should 'never give yourself a way out – failure is not an option'.

FEAR – FROM ONE CRUISING ALTITUDE TO THE NEXT

Can you believe you were once scared of water? Or even of getting your hair cut? Walking, which is one of life's most basic functions, was once a real threat to you. That is, until you decided to take that first step – and then, bang, you fell over! With a little bit of encouragement from your mum and dad, you persisted, and you haven't looked back since.

Fear of any challenge in your life is really there to stretch you, to take you from one comfort zone to the next. Think back to your first date and how nervous you were. It probably brings a smile to your face now, but back then you were so unsure of yourself – and that was okay. You have grown from that point. You challenged yourself, met the fear head on, and wow! You went on to more dates and developed relationships. Asking someone out or saying yes to a new person suddenly became a lot easier after that first time.

Think of a fear right now that could be holding you back from achieving more of your potential. Maybe it is speaking in front of your peers at work, or if you have mastered that, in front of an unknown audience. Take it from me – contrary to public opinion, great public speakers are not born to it.

They just practise a lot. If you can give yourself more opportunities to get up in front of an audience, you will find that you start to get more comfortable as your self-talk changes from 'I hate this' to 'I think I'm getting the hang of this – it's getting easier'. After more and more presentations, your self-talk goes even further, with comments like 'This is great', and 'They're really enjoying my presentation'.

When you challenge fear or pain in your life and meet it head on, you take away its hold on you. Mary Tyler Moore, one of the world's most enduring actors, once said of pain: 'How can you be courageous without having been through any challenges in life? It's the challenges in life that force us to draw out our courage'.

So the next time you're faced with a setback, always know that an equal or better opportunity is around the corner – but only if you think so.

FEELING DOWN? TRY THESE QUICK TIPS

Did you know that studies have shown that we all feel down at least eight times a day? This doesn't mean we walk around with our head bowed on each of the eight occasions, but it does alert us to the fundamental challenge that faces all of us, all the time – that we have to *work at* staying on top.

What determines how low you go each time you get upset is your level of self-esteem. Remember back in Chapter 2, when I talked about the Self-esteem Bank Account? If you can manage to keep topping up your account, you will find that you can always rally yourself when the going gets tough and things are not going your way.

As we saw earlier, Ken Tagg had to endure a great deal to get to where he is today. Knockbacks and setbacks are a part of life. And it's worth taking another look at what Anne Morrow Lindbergh says in her book, *Gift from the Sea*, about your whole life being like an ocean tide. When the tide is out and all seems lost, just hang in there, because the tide will come back.

Here are ten quick tips to remember when you're not feeling like the champion you really are:

1. Use the projection technique A favourite among sporting identities, the projection technique is simply concentrating on an enjoyable past event or achievement and rekindling the emotion that went with that event. For instance, you might have beaten the best swimmer in the school when you were twelve. The emotions you felt then will still be with you. By thinking back to that event, you can use all the positive emotions you experienced and project them into the current challenge facing you.

For example, when I am booked to speak to a group or industry which I have not worked with before, and find my self-talk doubting that I can deliver an excellent presentation, I simply go back to a recent presentation and remember the feedback I received at the end of it. I recall how great I felt that so many people were moved by what I had said. Then, when I feel the emotion, I start to think about the coming event and connect the emotion with it. *I am in the pilot's seat of my life.*

2. Rework your diary It's amazing how many clients or opportunities you have right under your nose. Grab your diary and look through the pages for the last twelve months. You will be struck by the amount of unfinished business. Write down ten contacts you have neglected and phone them tomorrow. This is one form of business generation that does not take any mental power.

3. Organise your files, or clean up the garage When you're feeling a bit off, one of the reasons might be your lack of accomplishment. Cleaning up your garage, pantry or office might sound trivial, but it will lift your spirits. How many times have you heard someone say, after a death in the family, that they 'threw themselves into their work' and felt better for it? Many times, you need something to break the current of bad energy to help your thinking back onto the winning and achievement track.

4. Listen to nature One of the most powerful 'healers' for anxiety is the sound of flowing water. An hour on the sand or in the pool does wonders. Another simple way to ease your worries is to go to your local park, lie down under a tree, look at the sky and listen to the birds. In a short while, the greenery and fresh air will improve your state of mind.

If it's not easy for you to get to a beach or park, there is an alternative. You can put on a relaxation or 'mood' recording. These recordings are specifically designed to help you relax. I didn't really believe they worked until I tried listening to a tape of beach sounds. At the time, I lived close to a national park, so I didn't really need a recording of birds singing –

I had this in my backyard. What I really enjoyed about the tape was the sound of waves crashing and seagulls crying overhead. I listened to this while my house was being cleaned, and it really relaxed me. In fact, my housekeeper commented on how calming it was compared to the Jimmy Barnes that I normally used as background music!

5. Plan a weekend escape We compare our setbacks to where we are heading. Maybe you have lost focus not on the bigger picture, but on your short-term goals. Plan something enjoyable about four to six weeks ahead and watch how your mood starts to improve.

Claudia, a successful salesperson, will vouch for the power of regular breaks. She told me that every New Year's Day, while all her friends are busy making ridiculous New Year's resolutions, she spends the day recovering and planning for a big new year ahead. Her plans always include four specific weekend breaks that are in addition to her annual leave. She said that she is amazed how, whenever something unpleasant happens in her day-to-day work or home environment, she finds herself thinking about the next break. Her 'weekend escape breaks', as she calls them, always recharge her batteries and provide time to refocus.

6. Read read read It's been said that knowledge is power. Give it a go and see why the cliché is true. Bryce Courtenay, the famous Australian author, has said that if you want to ensure your child gets a head start in life, forget the personal computer. Computers are only as smart as the person who is driving them. Bryce suggests that parents spend time reading to their kids, and have them read to them, to ensure an excellent vocabulary and general knowledge. From a personal perspective, I find the ultimate indulgence is flying from A to B with a great book. You can't beat the feeling. Try it next time you fly and you will be pleasantly surprised. The flight seems to go quicker as well!

7. Meditate Meditation is a very under-used relaxation tool. For some reason, many people still think that you have to be a member of some strange sect to meditate. Meditation simply quietens your thinking and puts you in touch with your thoughts and feelings.

How do you meditate? One way to learn is to buy one of the many books on the market which teaches meditation techniques. For example, a quick technique is given in Shakti Gawain's excellent book, *Creative Visualisation*. It's called the 'Pink Bubble Technique', and is easy to use and very effective. When you are worried about something and just don't know how to handle it, close your eyes and imagine a large pink bubble above your head. Enclosed in the bubble is your challenge or worry. Slowly imagine the bubble drifting high above you and going towards the sky with your challenge, taking it away from your conscious mind so that the sub-conscious mind can sort it out.

I have used this technique hundreds of times and found it to be not only relaxing but energy-boosting. Instead of worrying about something that might be out of my control, like a friend or relative who is going through tough times emotionally or financially, I start to work on things that I *can* control. It's great – give it a try.

There are some further suggestions for books on meditation in the reading list at the back of this book.

8. Catch up on your accounting Figures and accounting are usually not the forte of most people. But if you take some time to organise your finances, you will feel able to perform more demanding tasks. It's not that accounting competes with meditation in the relaxation stakes – it's more that when you do, say, an hour's work getting your figures in order, you at least feel you are accomplishing something. And let's face it, when you're down, you don't really want to talk to anyone. Accounting is a task you can do on your own, at your own pace.

9. Mix with positive people Try mixing with some positive people and see how your spirits lift. When you're not feeling on top of the world, you need positive people around you to help you back onto the right path. The cruel irony is that you attract to yourself whatever you feel you deserve. When you are down, you might feel that achievers or positive people are a 'threat'. Be aware of this. They are not being over-positive – it could be that you are feeling low. This is dangerous, because when you are down you will generally feel more comfortable with people who are down there with you.

10. Believe Believe in yourself and your innate potential and you will always pull through. How many times while you were growing up did something you were really worried about turn out all right? Maybe it was a huge decision like who you would invite to the school formal – a major decision for a teenager. Or maybe it was an argument you had with your brother which got out of hand and led to you not speaking to each other for a while. You thought you'd never make up, but you did, and now your relationship is the best it's ever been.

So if something is not right at the moment, either in your relationship or at work, sit tight. Don't let your imagination run wild with possible outcomes. Review your goals and stay focused.

> # Remember: focus on where you want to go, and never, ever give up.

DON'T QUIT

I can't tell you how many people have come up to me and said how much inspiration they get every time they read the poem called 'Don't Quit'. And I believe them, 100 per cent. In my early days, while I was struggling to build my business, this poem never left my side. In fact, some days I felt that it was the only thing that kept me going.

I hope you enjoy it and that it gives you as much inspiration as it has me and thousands of others worldwide.

Don't Quit
When things go wrong, as they sometimes will,
when the road you're trudging seems all uphill,
when the funds are low and the debts are high,
and you want to smile, but you have to sigh,
when care is pressing you down a bit –
rest if you must, but don't you quit.

Life is strange with its twists and turns,
as every one of us sometimes learns,
and many a person turns about

when they might have won had they stuck it out.
Don't give up, though the pace seems slow –
you may succeed with another go.

Often the goal is nearer than it seems
to a faint and faltering person;
often the struggler has given up
when they might have captured the victor's cup;
and they learned too late when the night came down
how close they were to the golden crown.

Success is failure turned inside out –
the silver tint of the clouds of doubt,
and you never can tell how close you are,
it may be near when it seems afar.
So stick to the fight when you're hardest hit –
it's when things seem worst that you mustn't quit.

WANT TO KNOW MORE ABOUT . . . ?	Turn to . . .
How your self-esteem shields you in adversity	Chapter 2
Why goal-setting makes you resilient	Chapter 4
The teacher arrives when the student is ready	Chapter 10
Commitment during the tough times	Chapter 2
Attracting the good things in life	Chapter 13
How mixing with positive people keeps you happy	Chapter 7
Believing in yourself more	Chapter 2

CHAPTER NINE

Forgive – and Heal Your Life

'No one can upset you unless
you give them permission.'

PAUL HANNA

IN THIS CHAPTER:

The person with the higher self-esteem apologises first

✳

When you apologise, you discard anger and
make room for happiness

✳

Regrouping after a divorce

✳

Dis-ease and unease towards others

✳

Forgiveness and how it heals us all

✳

Forgiving your parents for being human

✳

When you blame someone, you give them
power over you

C an you remember a time when you were hurt by someone close to you? Maybe it was a long-time friend. Or your partner. Or a close, trusted associate at work.

Whatever the incident, I want you to let it go for a while and, for the moment, try to become neutral to it. Not pretend it never happened – it's happened, and that's that. I want to share with you some very powerful examples of what happens when you take full accountability for your own happiness.

Apologising is tough for most of us. But what happens when you apologise even though you think you're in the right? Yes, that's right – *in the right!*

BROTHERLY LOVE? WELL, NOT QUITE ...

Reg, in his late forties, reacted very strongly to the point about apologising even though you're in the right during one of my presentations recently. He spoke of his relationship with his brother, Mel, who was about five years younger than him, and described the event which led to his not speaking to Mel for several years.

About six years ago, Reg lent Mel $10 000 so he could start a small business. Mel, who was sick and tired of working for a boss, wanted to try his hand at his own business, but what Reg didn't know was that, like so many others, he had failed to do research into its viability. A year later nearly to the day, he told Reg that he was struggling and wasn't sure whether he could repay the debt in the short term. He asked for some more time. The alarm bells started ringing for Reg. He knew this was the end of his $10 000. About six months later, he heard that Mel had gone into bankruptcy. To the day Reg came to my seminar, his brother had not rung or apologised for the situation.

When I asked Reg whether *he* had apologised to *Mel*, he could not believe my question. He said, 'I don't think you were listening, Paul', and started to tell me the story again. I interrupted him. If his brother had enough self-esteem, he would have apologised first. *The person with the higher self-esteem makes the first move to apologise.* I went on to ask Reg whether this incident had taken its toll on his health and happiness. He said that not only had *he* missed his brother and his family, his kids were also saying how much they missed their Uncle Mel and Aunt June and cousins.

Reg decided that he was going to make the first move to apologise to his brother, even though he knew he, Reg, had done nothing wrong. He realised that the trauma of losing everything they had, as well as the money borrowed from him, had really taken its toll on Mel and his family. They were at rock bottom both financially and emotionally.

At a follow-up seminar, Reg came up to me and told me how things had panned out. He was now back on speaking terms with his brother, and his kids were having the time of their life with their 'new' cousins. But most of all, Reg said that his own performance at work had improved dramatically, with everyone noticing his new outlook on life.

THE CALL TO THE IN-LAWS

Simon, a successful lawyer, came up to me at the end of a seminar. He had attended a previous seminar nine months earlier and wanted to tell me how much his life had changed since then – all because of one phone call. When I had shared the story of Reg in that first seminar, Simon told me he had felt I was talking directly to him.

His first marriage had ended in acrimony and he had not seen his two sons, now teenagers, for years. His relationship with his former wife was, to say the least, icy. Years had passed, and Simon had remarried, as had his first wife. She had custody of the boys. Simon had no problem with this, but he knew that he had let down not only her, but also their two sons. He had also been very close to his in-laws, who, in the fall-out, had suffered as well. Simon had not spoken to either of them for years.

He went on to tell me that he had been in poor health for two years. He missed his boys desperately and could not imagine never seeing them again. His second wife encouraged him to get back on speaking terms with them, because, if he did not, he would end up 'six foot under'. It was that bad.

It took him about two months to gather the courage to pick up the phone, but he finally did it. One Friday night, he phoned his in-laws and apologised for all the hurt he had created. He told them he knew that marriage was a two-way street, but that as a father and a husband, he had let everyone, including himself, down. The reaction from his in-laws was ecstatic. They could not talk to him enough and encouraged him to get back together with his boys. They also said their daughter was now coming to realise that she could be a little bit to blame too! Simon then told me that his life has totally changed. Not long after that phone conversation, he rang his first wife, and together they agreed that, not only for the boys' sake, but for their own sake, they had to sort things out emotionally. Simon's ex-wife arranged for her second husband to go away fishing for the weekend so that Simon and the in-laws, as well as the boys, could get together again, to start repairing the ties that were so badly damaged by the divorce.

Simon said that the events since that first seminar had totally changed his life. His new marriage was fantastic, his work performance was going through the roof, his health had improved dramatically and life in general looked great. At work, all his colleagues were quite amazed at how settled he was. He had started not only to act calmer, but also to look calmer. His face muscles had started to relax, and it showed. Simon said that he was still getting compliments from the people he worked with. Some of them couldn't put their finger on what had changed, and would say things like, 'You look different' and 'Have you been on holidays?'

DIS-EASE AND UNEASE

Have you heard the saying, 'Time heals all wounds'? In one sense this is true, but in another sense, time can actually be more destructive than healing.

Take Simon's story, for instance. He went for nearly five years carrying a pain that was like an infected sore. He kept on putting bandages on it, but the sore was there and no amount of covering it up was going to fix it. It was only when he started to examine it and treat it that the sore started to heal.

Most Eastern philosophies accept that all disease in your life is actually just that – dis-ease. In other words, you are not at ease, or you are uneasy, with something in your life.

How many people do you know who have been in an abusive relationship? They may not literally be being bashed every night – it could be that one partner feels so tormented by the lack of love in the relationship, and eventually comes to have such a lack of respect for themselves, that they find they are stuck in a relationship they no longer want to be in. Or the 'uneasy' relationship may be with someone else close to them, such as Simon and his ex-wife.

For many, the only way out of this type of relationship is through death. I don't mean suicide. Because of the unease they feel in their life, there is only one road left for them: a disease, which could be fatal.

The Chinese have long held the belief that cancer and anger are related, as are heart disease and forgiveness. In her very powerful book, *You Can Heal Your Life*, Louise Hay connects different types of illness or physical condition to our mental state. When you read about these connections for the first time, you may think she is over-generalising, but the more I hear about someone with an illness or disease, the more I refer back to these connections and, in the majority of cases, they are spot on.

For instance, asthma is connected with too much love, being smothered and not being able to 'breathe' for oneself. Back problems are connected to lack of emotional support (upper back), guilt (middle back) or fear of money (lower back), while being overweight is connected to a longing for protection. Colds represent too much going on in your life at once; migraines show a dislike of being told what to do and are also connected with sexual fears; and neck problems are related to flexibility.

I could fill this book with connections between your mental state and your physical well-being, but I just wanted to give you a few brief examples of how your thinking can affect who you become. If you want to know more about this area, get a copy of Louise Hay's book. It's great reading.

FORGIVE – AND HEAL YOUR LIFE

If you asked Reg and Simon who had benefited most from their making the first move to forgive, what do you think they would say to you?

Exactly! *They* had, of course. In any religion, forgiveness usually features somewhere. Why? Because of its healing quality. Think of the last time you were holding a grudge against someone close to you. A friend or relative, or maybe a work associate. Who ends up with the ulcer? Who ends up with the insomnia? Who ends up with the migraines?

Forgiveness is not only for the other person – more than anything else, it's for you. As we discovered earlier on, it's the person with the higher self-esteem who apologises first. When you lift your self-esteem you find it in your heart to forgive others, because you now have space for happiness. The anger and hatred have been kicked out of your heart and there is now space for joy and love. Remember your Self-esteem Bank Account? You can't give away something you don't have, so the first person to start with is yourself.

If this sounds a bit too 'feel-good' . . . well, it is! If you want to create space in your world for happiness and abundance, get rid of the anger now.

THE LETTER OF FORGIVENESS

You wouldn't have got this far in my book if you weren't serious. You mean business, so let's take action! Make a list of the people who you feel have hurt you in some way. These don't have to be recent events. It could be a past lover who dumped you. It could be a work colleague who was threatened by your quick rise up the ladder and who did the dirty on you.

Okay, now you've written your list I'm going to tell you that one of the quickest ways to let go of pain in your life is to write a letter to the person connected with that pain – but not to post it or give it to that person! In fact, as soon as you know that the pain is healed, you can throw the letter in the bin.

Look at your list and choose the person who you feel has hurt you the most. Now, just as you would write an ordinary letter to a friend, start writing whatever comes into your head. Don't think about it – just write.

Remember, no one is ever going to see it except you. In the letter, tell the person in the strongest terms how much they hurt you, or how bad you felt when they walked out, or how betrayed you felt when you were sacked.

After you have done this, put the letter in a safe place and leave it for a few days. Then re-read it and revise it until you are comfortable with the way you have told the story – this is what happened, no ifs or buts. This is it.

Now, the reason you wrote this letter is because you want to heal the pain in your world. Right? So next, write a 'healing' letter to the same person, letting them know that what happened happened, and you know they did it for their own self-protection. You now know that it was not your fault or mistake, and you understand that they did what they did to protect their own self-esteem, not to damage yours.

Remember: this letter is not to be given to the person under any circumstances. It's for you and your recovery.

Angry at Dad for Walking Out

Cathy, a marketing executive for a large firm, approached me at one of my seminars in Brisbane. She had heard me at a conference earlier that year and thought the 'letter of forgiveness' idea sounded a bit corny. Why write a letter if the other person would never see it? However, she had tried everything else to get over an incident in her past, so she thought she'd give the letter a go. What did she have to lose?

The incident in question had to do with her father. When Cathy and her brothers were aged twelve, eleven and nine, their father had walked out. 'We all thought we had done something to make him walk out. It happened at Christmas after a big fight between my mum and dad. As kids, we thought the cost of our Christmas presents was the cause, because mum and dad were always fighting about money. Now that I am married, I know his walking out had nothing to do with us kids, nor with money for that matter. It was all about self-esteem.'

Cathy continued: 'The more I listen to the tape you gave out at the end of your seminar, the more I feel sorry for dad and wish he had had self-help books and tapes like we have now to help him get his act together. I wrote a letter to him (the one you never post), and was amazed at how much emotion I felt as I was writing. I felt a massive amount of grief for myself, which changed to forgiveness for dad, because he did the best he could with the limited skills he had as the son of a miner in the 1950s.

'My dad now lives in the Northern Territory. I hadn't seen him for nearly four years, but a month ago I visited him in Darwin. He commented on how relaxed I looked and, out of the blue, started to apologise for what had happened all those years ago.'

A coincidence? I don't think so. Cathy said that, to this day, she has not shown the letter to her dad. She re-reads it whenever she realises she is feeling sorry for herself, or when she finds herself blaming her dad's past actions for something. 'It's one of those things that you have to actually experience yourself – put pen to paper and see how powerful it really is.'

RECLAIMING YOUR POWER

When you blame someone or something else, you give away your power to that person or event. When you carry the load of resentment, it's worse than carrying a sack of potatoes around all day. Slowly, day after day, you are going to be worn into the ground from fatigue, all because of an event that has happened which you think had nothing to do with you.

Take accountability for any incident that is wearing you down, and you'll see the solution. Put the blame on someone else and you become the victim.

WANT TO KNOW MORE ABOUT . . . ?	**Turn to . . .**
The teacher arrives when the student is ready	Chapter 10
Goal-setting and keeping focused	Chapter 4
Self-esteem and handling setbacks	Chapter 2
Why goal-setting makes you resilient	Chapter 4
Seeing greatness in others	Chapter 17
Dealing with negative people	Chapter 11

CHAPTER TEN

The Teacher Arrives When the Student Is Ready

'I know God will not give me anything I can't handle. I just wish that he didn't trust me so much.'

MOTHER TERESA

IN THIS CHAPTER:

You attract people and events to teach you

✳

You treat the world as you currently feel

✳

You can only get angry with yourself

✳

Every person you deal with reflects a part of you

✳

The teacher keeps on returning until
the lesson is learnt

✳

You can't change people – they are your teacher

✳

The teacher 'exercise'

O f all the material I share in my presentations, this chapter's contents – which I call 'The Teacher' – have had by far the most impact. As we learnt earlier on, 'Feedback is the breakfast of champions', and I have certainly had an enormous amount of feedback on 'The Teacher'. People always comment on how simple yet profound the message is, and gain a lot from it.

The basic idea of 'The Teacher' is part of many Eastern religions: 'The teacher arrives when the student is ready'. Put simply, this statement means that we attract in our life people, events and experiences to teach us. The universe delivers to us the 'teacher' when we are ready to learn.

Life is our teacher. It is the greatest university there is. But it can be the harshest teacher – I know that. For me, knowing that life is my teacher, and that I attract teachers to me to teach me different lessons, was a very empowering thing to learn. I now no longer feel like a victim of the events and people around me, because I know that I am in the pilot's seat of my life.

To really understand this principle, you need to accept that the world is your reflection and that you always see and experience the world based on how you feel at any given time. Have another look at 'The Man in the Mirror' in Chapter 2 to remind yourself of its message.

THE WORLD REFLECTS YOU AND HOW YOU FEEL

To put this very empowering information into perspective, just pretend that from now on, every person you meet, every incident that happens, is a reflection of something about you. When you fully grasp this concept, it raises you to a new level of understanding, not only of the people around you, but of yourself. Why? Because you will start treating the world and everyone in it according to the way you feel inside.

Let's put this up in lights!

You are currently treating the world the way you feel inside.

When you feel fantastic, you treat the world and everyone in it fantastically. When you feel lousy, you treat the world and everyone in it badly.

For example, using this principle, you can only really get angry at yourself, not at external things. If you have accepted that the world is your mirror, it's logical also to accept that when you get angry at anyone or anything, you are really getting angry at a part of yourself.

A RIGID TREE WILL ALWAYS BREAK

An ancient Eastern saying says: 'Only the trees that cannot bend will struggle when the strong wind arrives'. In other words, if you become too pedantic about something, you become rigid and therefore lose the ability of being flexible.

Take my attitude to time. The business world loves my attitude to time. It rewards it very handsomely and respects me for it. Being on time is not only good business practice, it is also common courtesy. However, when it gets to an obsessive level, it's not healthy. Putting too much emphasis on it can lead to distress.

Come in, teacher – or, in this case, client. In the past, when I was being pedantic about time, I would always attract a 'teacher' who said 'Take it easy' or 'Relax'.

The One that Got Away

My most recent 'teacher' arrived while I was writing this book. I had just finished a speaking engagement for a senior management team at an early-morning breakfast meeting, and it had gone extremely well. The Managing Director was thrilled with the outcome and arranged to engage me to share my material with the remainder of his staff. I was firing. Things were rolling.

Following on from the breakfast, I had a meeting with someone who had been referred to me by a long-term client who had enjoyed my seminars and was certain that the person he had referred me to was keen to use my services. Because of the success of the breakfast meeting, I was delayed in getting to the appointment. I rang from my car to let the new client, James, know that I was on my way, and apologised. (Of course, this was the natural thing to do.) I arrived about fifteen minutes late and quickly made my way to his office.

When I arrived, James was meeting with one of his staff. Seeing me in the lounge area, he came out and said that he had a phone call to take because it was the 'end of the month', and would I mind waiting five minutes. I said, 'Of course not. Go ahead.' Five minutes turned into ten minutes, which turned into twenty and then, eventually, thirty. I was fuming. How could he keep me waiting? I was translating his keeping me waiting into a snub.

I got up, furious because of the delay, but not showing how angry I was. I walked into his office and said, 'Excuse me, James. I think I will come back another time.' He said he was sorry, but the figures had to come first. Then I stuffed it up big-time. I said, 'Well, the least you could have done is keep me informed on the delay.' At this point, *he* got angry.

He said, 'If you can't wait, then leave.' And then, 'On second thoughts, let's forget the whole thing.'

I left in a really confused state. How could he keep me waiting so long and then blame me? It's amazing what ten minutes of driving can do – I calmed down and decided to ring James and apologise. When I phoned he told me that the Managing Director had been on the phone to him, grilling him about the figures. It was pressure time for him and he thought I should have had a bit more empathy.

And he was right. I stuffed up. Do you know why? Comfort zones. My self-talk was going crazy, saying all sorts of things like: 'How could he?' and 'Why won't he come out and explain?'

The bottom line is, no one can upset you unless you give them permission. Remember reading that in Chapter 2? I gave away my power, and accused him of upsetting me, when really it was my past conditioning about punctuality that had caused me to 'carry on' like that. That lost business was one of the best lessons I had learnt in a long time. I saw in a very painful way how we only get angry at ourselves.

Was there a lesson for me? You bet there was! Two months later, I was in a similar situation to the one I had with James, which could have turned just as negative. What had happened earlier popped into my mind again. But this time I knew how to react – it was so clear now. When the client I was visiting was delayed for forty-five minutes, I pulled out the book I had in my bag and lost myself in it. When my client was finally ready, I was relaxed, and he was apologetic. He felt bad for keeping me waiting, and guess what? I got the business!

WE ATTRACT PEOPLE WE NEED TO LEARN FROM

Have you ever wondered why, out of eighteen million people in Australia, you met the person who is now your partner and why you both decided to get together? One of the hardest things many people face in life is the reality that the relationship they thought would go on forever is now faltering and going nowhere. The sad days are starting to outnumber the good days, and the couple are questioning whether it's all worthwhile.

Let me take you back to Sun Tzu's *The Art of War*, which I referred to in Chapter 4. When you leave no escape route in your relationship, you make it work, through thick and thin. Have you seen the movie *When a Man Loves a Woman*, with Meg Ryan and Andy Garcia? It's about a woman who is an alcoholic and her successful husband who tolerates the situation. The movie focuses on how the woman recognises that she has a problem and admits herself to a drug and alcohol rehabilitation clinic in the hope that she can recover. But what both husband and wife learn is that *he* is just as much a part of the problem as she is. He needs her to be constantly getting drunk so he can 'rescue' her and thereby retain his role as the powerful partner in the relationship.

What would happen if she did not need the drink to lift her spirits? What would happen to their relationship if she could improve her self-esteem? He discovers that, like all of us, you attract everyone in your life to teach you a lesson. He learnt that he needed her to stay fixed to the addiction so he would continue to feel in control.

The film asks a brilliant question: who needs help – the addict or the partner, or both? The film ends with the wife taking responsibility for her life, and for the fact that their relationship, if it is going to survive, will have to be on the basis of their roles in it being equal, not a 'victim' and a 'rescuer'.

The world is full of sayings which ask you not to judge other people. 'The person who has not sinned, throw the first stone.' 'Walk a mile in another Indian's moccasins before you make judgement.' What would happen if you let go of trying to change everyone and started to ask questions such as: 'I wonder what I could learn from this person or event'?

We attract in our life people and things we feel we deserve.

In a consulting session, I was discussing a business decision with a client, Carl. He suddenly changed tack and asked what I thought about his having been married three times and contemplating number four. I said that it was none of my business and wished him all the best.

He kept on with the subject and said, 'If there was one piece of advice you could give me about my pending marriage, what would it be?' I said that he should understand that he is attracting in his life people and events that mirror his self-esteem. When he decides to lift his self-esteem, he will attract different people.

I asked him if he wanted to make the marriage work – seemingly a ridiculous question. Carl answered 'Of course I do!' I said that if he didn't want to end up at marriage number five, he needed to accept that this partner was for life, and that at the most negative times of their marriage, when things seemed hopelessly damaged, he would need to remember that we attract in our life people who we feel we are worthy of. He is with his wife-to-be because she can teach him the lessons he most needs to learn.

After discussing his past marriages, Carl agreed that they had all ended because of his unwillingness to spend his hard-earned money. His lesson was that he needed to ease up on his bank account a little. But instead of accepting this, he let go of three wives. The irony, Carl said, was that he has now paid out heaps of money in settlement to his ex-wives.

After our discussion, Carl was amazed that something that had had so much impact on his life could be staring him in the face and yet he couldn't see it. He realised that his beliefs about himself were getting in the way of a happy relationship.

Carl is no different to any of us. We all have beliefs that we have picked up as we have travelled through life, and it is these beliefs that sometimes get in the way of our happiness and success.

YOU CHOOSE TO WORK WHERE YOU WORK

Your self-esteem governs what you attract in life. You know that now. But what about where you work and who you work with? Could your self-esteem limit you in the workplace? Of course it could.

We all decide where we want to work. If things aren't going well there, we either decide to stay and put up with the problems, or we leave. But an amazing thing happens when we lift our self-esteem. We start to enjoy our work more, we start to enjoy our workmates' company more and, most of all, we get on better with everyone.

The Teacher Keeps Visiting Until the Student Has Learnt

All of us have to move on at some stage. In fact, to stay in the one job for a long time could mean you have run out of goals in your life. But what happens when things are not going right and you get the urge to move to something better? I once heard a saying, 'If the grass is greener on the other side, water your own lawn'!

You discovered earlier on that every person you meet or come in contact with mirrors a part of you. So what if there is someone at work that really gets up your nose? Well, as painful as it may be, they have something to teach you. The interesting point here is this. If you say 'I don't need someone like that creep to teach me', what do you think eventually happens? You keep on attracting people that are similar to the 'creep' at work because, whatever it is, you have not learnt the lesson.

Ben, a senior executive with a computer firm, told me that he had seen this principle demonstrated in his life. He had left his previous job because of a problem with his expense account. When I met him he had been in his new job for six months, and the same problem had surfaced again.

In his old job, Ben had travelled frequently and was always billing things to the company account. The financial controller was always 'at' Ben to put in receipts for his expenses. Company policy for everyone, including the managing director, was that receipts had to be included in expense claims or there would be no payment. Ben said that he had kept on bucking the system until the financial controller sent him a terse memo outlining the current terms of his employment. In other words, Ben received a 'letter' to lift his game or else. Ben couldn't believe it. How could his company not trust him?

Ben eventually left the company because he was 'sick and tired' of the paperwork that was required. In his new job, guess what popped up? You got it – expense-account receipts. The company accountant said that it was not a matter of trust, it was a matter of company policy, and if he didn't like it he could leave. Full stop.

Ben said that while the system was a nuisance, he realised he had to accept that this was worldwide business practice and that if he kept on quitting companies over expense-account problems, he would eventually get a reputation as someone who was fiddling his expenses. This was not true, but what would *you* think if you heard that someone had left two companies over problems with his expense account? The first thing you'd think of would be fraud. An ounce of image is worth a ton of performance!

A Lost Contract – He Asked for It!

One of the most telling examples of how our thinking affects the people around us is best described by something I witnessed about two years ago. A close friend and business associate, Justin, had confided in me that he was just about to land a very profitable and exciting contract with a mining company. After we had discussed the amount of time and effort that went into obtaining the account, I asked who he would be working with in the company. (I always ask this question, because it really determines how successful you are going to be in that environment.)

Justin said that the guy he would be working closely with was a wimp and he didn't really know how he had got as far as he had in the mining business. I was astonished at this comment! We all give out an 'aura' which can dramatically affect how people see us and, more importantly, feel towards us. I wanted to tell Justin he was heading for disaster with this attitude, but as often happens when you try and give friends advice, I knew he wouldn't take it very well. So I was a bit more tactful, and said that if he was to make the account work, he'd better start thinking more positively towards his client or things might start to go downhill. (Remember the witch's hat in the driving-school example in Chapter 4? We move in the direction we are looking at.)

About six months passed, and I met Justin at a fundraising dinner. As the night progressed, I enquired how the account was going. He became a bit defensive and said 'All right!' I could see immediately that the account had stalled. After about half an hour of excuses for why it had not gone well, Justin admitted that one of the major reasons was that his relationship with his contact in the organisation, the guy he had called a 'wimp' six months earlier, had deteriorated to the point that phone calls were not returned and everything became really difficult. Eventually, while the organisation honoured the work they currently had with him, they began not to renew contracts – a sure sign that something was wrong.

Justin had realised that now, more than at any other time in his career, he was losing many clients, not by the way he was doing his actual business deals, but by his opinions of them during and after the deal.

Justin commented to me later that he wondered how many clients he was losing because of his attitude, but that he was glad to accept accountability. He knew that if he didn't, the 'teacher' – his clients getting vibes that he only wanted their money and didn't really think much of them personally – would keep revisiting until he learned his lesson.

If your work environment is not very good at the moment, have a close look at your self-esteem. How do you feel about yourself? The world is really just reflecting back to you what you are currently thinking.

If there is a person at work you really can't stand, have a look at what you dislike about them. You'll find it's that which you see in yourself. If it wasn't, it wouldn't bother you – it would go right over your head, no worries. That's why, when I hear a person say, 'That guy really makes me sick' or 'If only you knew my wife, mate', I usually follow up with the line, 'So tell me, what is it that you most dislike about them?' After they have finished describing all the things they can't stand, I ask them to see if there is anything they need to learn from their teacher (i.e. that guy, or their wife). After a little hesitation, they usually realise what they can learn and where they can take more accountability for the way things are.

When you blame, you give away your personal power. When you take accountability for the way things are in your life, you empower yourself.

> # The people you most want to change have the greatest lesson for you.

WHO IS YOUR TEACHER?

In my case, I found that one of the most powerful lessons I ever learnt was staring me in the face – but I needed someone else's perspective to be able to see it.

I was at a party with some friends and we were all having a good time. However, our host always seemed to be fussing about the food, or changing the music, and not talking to us. I insisted that he relax a bit, because while the food was important, we, the guests, were more important. On the way home with a friend, I was complaining about our host neglecting us and she hit right back with, 'You do that sometimes!'

'What do you mean?' I said.

'You do just what he was doing,' she accused me.

'What – stuff around in the kitchen while all the guests are chatting away? I have never done that!'

'No,' she smiled. 'You don't do it at home; you sometimes do it at your seminars.'

'How?' I said.

She replied, 'When you are busy setting up the seminar room, you forget that the people outside waiting to come in are anxious and could do with a little chat before it starts. This is your teacher, Paul!'

Bang! Right between the eyes!

How can you find out who *your* teacher is? Make a list of the five people you would most like to change and the trait about them that irks you the most. Then have a think about what you've written and see if the fault actually lies within *you*, not them.

You may find it best to do this with a good friend or your partner, because it can help to have someone to point out things that might look a bit hazy to you or that you don't want to admit to yourself. But I have to warn you: you might learn some uncomfortable things about yourself. However, if you choose to do it with a good friend or partner, they should have your best interests at heart.

It's crazy when you think about it. We all journey through life wanting basically to be happy. We want to have as few hassles as possible and enjoy life as much as we can. So we are always searching for ways to achieve this. But as you have just seen, the answer could be right in front of you.

CHAPTER ELEVEN

Dealing with Negative People

'The more someone tells you how great
they are, the less they believe it.'

PAUL HANNA

IN THIS CHAPTER:

Negative people and self-esteem

❋

How negative people scream for help

❋

How a 'big-headed' person could have
low self-esteem

❋

Lower altitudes and negative people

❋

Why negative people need more positive feedback

I know that many people come to my seminar thinking, 'Here we go again – another hyped-up speaker.'

Knowing this only makes me want to give more. The more I see someone in the audience acting defensively, the more it rallies me to work harder to convince that person they have a lot more to give. When I talk about achieving more in life, these people will often come back with 'I'm quite happy with what I've got, thanks – I don't need to improve.' When I get comments like this, I know they really want to hear more.

If you're sitting there thinking, 'This guy has lost it', let me explain. As I said earlier, every salesperson, worldwide, knows the following quote and how true it is: 'An objection is a request for more information'. That is, customers – you and I – usually make a few negative comments to a salesperson before they actually start to get in the frame of mind to buy. Sales trainers agree that most buyers give up to eight objections before they start saying yes. *Eight* objections – yes, you read that right.

Successful salespeople know that if they persist and ask questions, they will eventually find out what information the customer wants to know about the product. Or the customer may simply have a list of requirements, and if these can't be satisfied, they won't be purchasing the product. The salesperson's role, of course, is to convince the customer that the product *can* do the job and won't let them down. Eventually, after all the objections the customer has made are answered, the time is perfect for the salesperson to ask for the sale. If the customer responds with 'I want to think about it', the salesperson knows that the customer has a few more questions to ask.

NEGATIVE PEOPLE ARE SCREAMING FOR HELP

Why am I telling you all this stuff about customers in a chapter about negative people? Because dealing with negative people in your life is the same as selling. You have an idea or service that you must sell to earn money to pay your mortgage or buy food or live your preferred lifestyle. Convincing negative people is the same. You have to start out with the goal – that you can convince them they can be positive – and know that people who are negative are really just not very sure of themselves. Forget about all their bravado and strong words – the bottom line is that they are scared inside and the way they keep people from getting too close is to keep everyone at a distance by being negative.

Another kind of person who needs your help is the 'big-noter'. There is a saying: 'The harder you try, the more doubt you imply'. This means that the person in your office who is constantly saying how great he or she is, is really not convinced of it. They are really asking for reassurance from the world that they are okay. It's easy to be put off by people like this and say, 'They have the biggest ego in the world. There is no way I'm going to tell them they did something great this afternoon. If I do, they won't be able to fit their head through the doorway, it'll be so big.' This could not be further from the truth! These people lack a real, deep-down belief in their own ability and are asking for reassurance because when they look at themselves, their Self-esteem Bank Balance is pretty low.

Help Them Lift Their Self-esteem

The best way I know to stop people being negative around you is to get them to start talking about a recent success, and reaffirm it to them. As you do this, think about their Self-esteem Bank Balance and ask yourself what you could do to assist this person to feel better about themselves. As they start to feel more confident, their negativity will start to drop away. And this will make your life easier!

Whether I am giving a one-hour keynote presentation or a full-day seminar, I always notice that the most successful people in the room are very self-assured; they know they are okay. They are a complete contrast to the people who are not confident: these people are extra-nervous and display body language to match: folded arms, no eye contact etc. What usually happens during the seminar is that the people who are self-assured will try to contribute to the seminar, and assist in whatever way they can to make the day a success. If I bring up an issue, they always try to give me a springboard to make me look good.

And what do the negative people attempt to do? You have most probably guessed already – they betray their lack of self-confidence by trying to bring everyone else down to their altitude. But as the seminar progresses, and they begin to enjoy the content – and, most of all, start to feel safe with me – I see a change in the way they sit. They no longer fold their arms, their gaze becomes steady, and they start to smile. It's a great feeling for both the participant and myself.

On countless occasions I have had people come up to me and say that they really didn't want to come to the seminar. They came because they had to – the boss said so. But what a buzz when they tell me they enjoyed the session, and describe which part they got the most out of.

Everyone has the ability to turn people around like this, but first you have to believe you can do it. As is true in every part of life, you can't give away something you don't have. It's simple: if you don't possess confidence yourself, how can you make other people feel confident? Your belief in yourself will determine how successful you are in turning a negative person around to a positive outlook. In fact, your level of self-confidence will determine how negatively you see people. Remember the quote in Chapter 2: 'The world is my mirror'? By lifting the balance in your own Self-esteem Bank Account, you start to see a world that is coloured by how you feel about yourself.

Have a look at your workplace. Everyone there is coping with changes in work practices – but, like you, they are probably also experiencing change in their personal life, whether it is a divorce, the sickness of a close friend or family member, the death of a loved one or, as is happening more and more these days, financial problems. Personal crises like these can show up at work in people's negative, arrogant or petty behaviour. How much empathy you display and how tolerant you are towards these people will usually depend on how smoothly you are handling your own challenges.

SETTING AN EXAMPLE

For some reason, we always tend to associate the word 'leadership' with corporate leadership. But what about leadership among colleagues at work? Or even among siblings at home?

Tess, who came up to me after a keynote presentation in Fiji, was a good example. She was going very well at work, and was excited to have been awarded this incentive to attend the course in Fiji. Tess said that the area of my presentation she found most helpful was the part on dealing with negative work colleagues. She said that, while she gets on well with everyone at work, she is irritated by one of her co-workers, who continually brags about how great she is at this and that.

'While we all try very hard to ignore the bragging, it always becomes too much for someone, and eventually they cut her down to size. However, your point, "The harder they try, the more doubt they imply", really fits our situation. I see now that what she is trying to do is to get us to acknowledge her work and think that she's okay – part of the team etc.

'I keep on seeing your Self-esteem Bank Account example and connecting it with her. I think she really needs our help to feel part of the team.'

Tess phoned me a month later to say that building this person up and helping her deposit a few points in her Self-esteem Bank Account has really paid dividends. The colleague is now more focused and confident and more relaxed with her work. The spinoff, Tess said, was that 'The group could have done this a lot earlier if we had seen her as the mirror. In other words, we thought *she* had the problem, but in a sense, it was our whole department's problem.

'We were not praising each other enough for the work we were doing, and instead of just praising the colleague with low self-esteem, we made a commitment that we would start to give feedback to each other as much as possible. Hopefully the collective self-esteem of the group will lift and our productivity will soar.'

It's pretty easy to see how you could translate this idea to your home situation, if there's a partner or child there who needs building up. If you need to brush up on this point, try a quick re-visit to Chapter 2 and the section on self-confidence.

CHAPTER TWELVE

Empowerment, or How to Motivate Others

'Give a person a fish, and you will
feed them for a day. Teach them
how to fish, and you feed them for life.'

ANCIENT EASTERN QUOTE

IN THIS CHAPTER:

When you give answers, you take away
another person's power

＊

Asking questions ignites focus

＊

How to make people independent,
not dependent on you

＊

How to stop kids and staff asking silly questions

＊

Goals, not gifts, motivate kids

L ast summer, one of my clients called me. 'Do you do any consulting with kids?' Don yelled down the phone. 'I want you to consult with my son.'

This was a first. I had given occasional seminars to teenagers and spoken to young employees in major corporations, but I had never consulted one-on-one with a child. Don was one of my major clients and had been impressed by the success I had had with his management team. Now he wanted to see if his son could be given similar assistance in achieving *his* goals. This is how he described him: 'Christopher is a loser. I've given him everything – private-school education, new cars, trips away – and I'm sick of it. It's about time he started to earn a living himself.' And how old was Don's 'kid'? Twenty-eight!

I said I would take Christopher to lunch and see what was going on. After two meetings, I rang Don and said, 'Can I come and see you?'

'What's the story?' he yelled.

'Well,' I replied, 'your son has a lot of potential, but there are a few things getting in the way.'

'Like what?' said Don.

'Like you', I said.

He didn't take kindly to my response. 'What do you mean?' he said.

'Well, every time he falls over, you're there to pick him up. He doesn't think he can do anything without you. Let go for a while. Stop making him like you. Let him be himself.' I explained that every time you give people the easy way out of their problems, you take a piece of their power away.

ASK QUESTIONS, DON'T GIVE ANSWERS

During a seminar I gave for a major pharmaceutical company, one of the senior managers said that she had once worked as a counsellor for Lifeline. The staff were drilled never to give answers over the phone when someone rang up distressed. This struck me as quite odd – I thought that's what their job was: to give answers.

The manager went on to explain what their role was really all about. She said that as much as possible, they asked questions. This, she said, would get the person on the other end of the line to think about their situation in a positive way instead of seeing themselves as a helpless victim. The last thing the staff wanted to do was let the person on the phone feel that they couldn't even come up with solutions. The manager went on to say that in most of the cases, if the right questions were asked, the person would come up with their own version of what they thought they could do to fix what was going wrong in their life.

After she had shared this fascinating insight, it dawned on me that this is exactly what sales professionals are taught day in and day out: 'Ask questions'.

How Questions Ignite Focus

It's very tempting to give people the answers to their problems, especially if they are less experienced in the subject in question than you are. But when you give people answers, you make them dependent on *you*, not dependent on themselves. Whether it's a problem specific to work or something more general, the same principle applies: if you give them the answers, they will keep on running back.

> When you solve people's problems for them, you take away their power.

In my corporate seminars, I can see the confusion in many audience members' eyes when I say that their job is not to give the answers, but to ask great questions. Not just any questions, *great* questions. Let me give you an example.

It's Mac Time Wow!

McDonald's are so far in front in their field that they could easily become arrogant and complacent. But instead, they have embraced my seminars with heaps of professionalism and enthusiasm – so much so that I still shake my head in wonder. It's only when you get close to the actual people behind the scenes at McDonald's that you realise how good they really are at what they do.

McDonald's has become part of mainstream Australian life, whatever you think about their food. This organisation employs kids straight out of school and turns them into focused, accountable and dynamic businesspeople. Over 3000 people at McDonald's Australia have attended the Paul Hanna Seminar, and the irony is, they did not need to attend. Yes, you read right. They did not *need* to attend, they *wanted* to attend. There's the difference.

In one of my McDonald's seminars, an assistant manager, Kate, asked me how she could stop her staff asking silly questions that she knew they could solve if they just thought about it a bit more. Why did they always come in and ask her opinion?

For the most part, when staff – or kids for that matter – are always asking for answers, it simply means they don't have the confidence to make a decision and live with it. They might know the answer. They might have had all the right training. But the bottom line is that if they don't think they have the correct answer, they will always check with you to ensure they are on the right path. That's great – if that's what you want.

But let's have a look at the mistake some managers and parents make when they get approached for the answer. Usually, to speed things up and because you know what the outcome will be, you give them the easy way out. You tell them what to do. They leave with the answer, but they also leave with the knowledge that when they have another curly problem, they know who to go to. You. Why? Because you have conditioned them to keep coming back for more.

Dependent or Independent?

What do smart leaders know? In the home or at work, the same principle applies: 'Come back later with three solutions'.

After we discussed her challenge, Kate realised that because she had come up the ranks in McDonald's she had seen it all before, and therefore found it easy to supply the answers. But this is not leadership. After a lengthy discussion, she saw that she should ask for more involvement from her crew.

Back at work, the next time one of her crew came in with a question, she asked them to come back in about ten minutes with three solutions they thought would fix their problem. Happy to have their manager solve all their problems, this came as quite a shock initially, but as you will see, her crew boomed and so did her McDonald's store.

'They are loving it', she said excitedly down the phone to me. What she found was that, after some initial trepidation, her crew realised they had most of the answers but were looking for coaching. She said she was amazed at how many times they now came in with one or two solutions to their problems. No longer did they come in empty-handed. They came in with what they knew was the right answer, and after they okayed it with her, they would go ahead.

Three weeks later, I had another call from Kate. A fascinating thing had happened – her crew were no longer even coming in and asking for her okay. They were just doing it!

QUESTIONS ARE POWERFUL – THEY EMPOWER

When we tell people how to do something, we take away their power. They have no investment in the outcome – it's *your* outcome. This is true in business or at home, with friends, family or business colleagues. The way to motivate the people around you is to ask them more questions. Let's have a look at two different scenarios.

Think for a moment about a recent social function you attended. Did you meet anyone special? Did you enjoy speaking with them? Most often, you remember fondly the person who asked questions about you, who was interested in what you were getting up to, how your business was going, what you thought of a recent news item or sporting event. They got you to talk and talk, and before you knew it, you had been chatting for about an hour but it felt like five minutes.

Now think of the last time you went to a party and the person you were sitting next to was boring. They were probably the one doing all the talking. They told you how their life was going (or wasn't going), what they thought of a current news item and what they thought was going to happen in the footy. No connection. No wonder!

To be the life of the party in either business or social environments, ask questions! It never fails.

GOALS, NOT GIFTS, MOTIVATE KIDS

Think back to the father-and-son case I related at the start of this chapter. In that situation, Don was always rescuing his son, to the point where Christopher became so dependent that he couldn't make any decision on his own.

You might be wondering what happened after my second phone conversation with Don. Well, he wasn't happy, and he let me know this in no uncertain terms. I told him he was paying me to give him good advice. It's interesting to note that when I asked Don whether anyone else had ever told him what I had, he said that the subject had only ever come up once. He had been at a convention in Singapore, and after a few drinks too many, one of his managers had said straight out that Don should let his son be himself and not try to run his life as much as he was. Nearly everyone in Don's corporation already knew that this was true, but because job security was more important to them than giving the boss some father/son advice, he was blind to what was so obvious to everyone else.

About three weeks passed, and Don went on one of his regular trips to the USA. I thought I would let him calm down a bit and then contact him on his return – but I didn't have to. Very early one morning, I heard my home fax screeching. This was unusual, because not many people know this particular fax number. I was curious. I got out of bed and walked to my study to see a fax coming through from New York.

It was from Don. He had seen a plaque in an airport gift shop, bought it, photocopied it and then faxed it to me. This is what he had written at the top: 'Paul, I thought about what you said. You did get through. Thought you might like to see this plaque!'

> # Don't give your kids
> # Cash and things,
> # Just give them
> # Goals for wings!

Kids, staff, adults: we are all the same. Once we have the confidence to make a decision, and trust ourselves, we just do it. Anyone who is constantly asking for reassurance needs to be convinced that they have got what it takes. That they can do it!

CHAPTER THIRTEEN

Attracting the Good Things in Life

'It is a funny thing about life:
if you refuse to accept anything but
the best, you very often get it.'

W. SOMERSET MAUGHAM

IN THIS CHAPTER:

Family conditioning and money

✳

How attitude and your bank balance are connected

✳

How comfortable are you with other people's success?

✳

New wealth-creating statements

✳

Quality really is everything

✳

A lesson on scrimping – it's expensive!

✳

How giving and receiving are the same thing

✳

How security is a state of mind

✳

Why money by itself doesn't take away fear

You learnt in Chapter 4 that you move in the direction of your thoughts. Your attitude towards money, and how much of it you attract in your life, are connected to this concept. If you move in the direction of your thoughts, then your current lifestyle reflects your current thinking. If you're not satisfied with that lifestyle, maybe you need to take a good look at how you currently think about money and success.

WHAT DID YOU PICK UP AT THE DINNER TABLE?

Of all the attitudes we pick up from our family, I believe our way of thinking about prosperity and abundance is the most remarkable. Try to remember what you heard around the dinner table when you were growing up concerning money; anything to do with money – saving, spending . . . Did you discuss the neighbours' financial position (or lack of position!)? What was said when someone close to the family bought a new car? Were there compliments all round or were there snide remarks insinuating that the person obtained the money in a negative way? Or maybe they were called a 'show-off' or a 'poser'.

In the 1970s and 1980s, Australia went through a boom period of house extensions. Can you remember what was said when one of your neighbours added another storey to their property? Were they congratulated? Or did you hear comments like 'What do they need all that space for?'

Take some time right now to write down some of the ones you can remember. To help you with this evaluation of your current thinking, here are some typical comments about money and success that I consider to be negative:

They are filthy rich.

All rich people are crooked or into drugs.

Money is the root of all evil.

I would prefer to be poor and happy than rich and lonely.

We Joneses have always struggled.

We're poor but at least we have our health.

You have to cheat to have money.

Starting today, for the next week try to be very aware of what you say to yourself. Be aware also of what you say out loud to your friends whenever you see a 'successful' person who seems to be doing better than you are, for example, someone driving a great car or living in an expensive house.

When you become aware of what you are saying and thinking, you will realise how you are pulling yourself down in the process. Once you are aware, you can re-program your self-image or autopilot to reflect your new altitude by changing the things you say and think.

NEW WEALTH-CREATING STATEMENTS

Remember the autopilot on the 747? It is controlling the height you are flying at. But you can lift your altitude about anything provided you take accountability to do so. If you want to attract more good things in your life, write down these positive statements and repeat them on a regular basis, say once a week:

I attract an abundant and prosperous lifestyle.

I see a world full of potential and excitement.

Money is my friend.

I love seeing people do well.

I attract only excellence in my life.

The statements I have given here are in *my* words, and are meant as a guide only. To achieve real impact for yourself, it is better to re-write them in your own words, words that will carry the most impact for you. Remember: *words trigger pictures in your mind, which then trigger emotions.*

Tips for Attracting the Good Things in Life

When I am presenting this module in my seminar, many people in my audience share how they prepare themselves for abundance and prosperity. Here are a few tips:

- Record your voice and listen to it repeating some of the above statements as you fall asleep. This is a very powerful time for all of us and the most receptive time for goal-setting.
- Write the statements on a small card and place it in a strategic location, for example in your wallet or purse, and look at it often.
- If you have an ensuite bathroom, place your statements on the rear of your toilet door. That way, only you and your partner will see them.
- Stick your statements on the ceiling above your bed, so they are the first things you see in the morning and the last things you see at night.
- Put a postcard of your holiday destination on the fridge. Take down old postcards of previous holidays and those which other people have sent you.

There are more tips in Chapter 4.

Your Income Mirrors Your Expectations

You probably know the saying, 'Which comes first – the chicken or the egg?'. I think many people face this dilemma when it comes to saving their money or building wealth. Some think that if they save and save, they will then have enough for their goals, but many fail to realise that their expectations of what they think they deserve to receive in life could be holding them back.

When you lift your expectations of what you think is good enough for you in life, you then set rolling a chain of events that will propel you to a new level of income. I have seen this in my own life over and over again. As soon as I commit to a goal, such as a trip overseas or a new car, suddenly a new client who wants to commit to new business comes along, seemingly out of the blue.

Your expectations, or 'prosperity consciousness', are the key to unlocking your potential and allowing you to see what is most probably right in front of you.

> # We move in the direction of our most prominent thoughts.

HOW COMFORTABLE ARE YOU WITH OTHER PEOPLE'S SUCCESS?

I will never forget what happened to a good friend of mine, Colin, when we were out to dinner with one of his clients. Colin bumped into an old work colleague, Trevor, who had been dismissed years ago, when they were both in sales together. After the usual 'You're looking good – what's happening?' conversation, Colin asked him how business was going. The guy who had been fired for incompetence five years before was now running his own marketing consultancy and doing very well for himself. He said that after the first three years of struggle, the business was now profitable and on its feet. Knowing that Trevor was a car buff, Colin asked him what car he was driving. He replied proudly that he had just bought a brand-new red Ferrari. Colin's response to this amazed me. Instead of congratulating Trevor, he changed the subject and totally ignored what was a big achievement. To me, this showed that Colin was uncomfortable with Trevor's success.

How comfortable you are with other people's success and wealth will determine what you attract in your own life. Have a good look at the statements you wrote and make a firm decision that if you ever find yourself repeating them, you will immediately change them to more positive statements. Eventually, with focus on your goals, you will find yourself becoming more comfortable with success.

Remember back in Chapter 1, when we discussed how your attitude determined your altitude? You did not know it as a kid, but a lot of the information given to you then was 'junk information', and this has influenced your current attitudes.

If you are aware you could have collected some misinformation along the way, then take accountability and change it. As I said earlier, your parents did the best they could with the knowledge they had – there weren't many self-development books and seminars around in their day. Now it's time to replace their outmoded information with new and more relevant information.

GOURMAND OR GOURMET?

The French, known the world over for their uncompromising desire for style and quality, have a great saying. They say that we all live our life with two choices: gourmand or gourmet.

I can hear you saying 'What on earth does gourmand mean?'! Most of us have a pretty good idea what 'gourmet' means, at least in the eating sense. It refers to someone who loves food and goes for quality. In contrast, a 'gourmand' also loves food but doesn't care what kind – anything will do, and the more the better. But these words can be used in a general sense, too. Very simply, gourmands choose to lead their lives with plenty of everything, but not much quality. Heaps and heaps of food, but not of a high standard. Plenty of shoes, but no real shoe of quality. Plenty of clothes, but again, not much of quality.

On the other hand, the gourmet focuses not on having lots and lots, but on having a limited amount of something while focusing on quality instead of quantity.

Quality Is Everything

Can you remember the last time you purchased a piece of clothing that did not perform up to expectations? Or an electrical appliance that kept on breaking down?

It's amazing how early the seeds of expectation are planted in our minds. I was always conditioned to pay that little bit extra, if it meant better quality. Ron and Julianne agreed with me on this – they had learnt their lesson on quality the hard way.

After saving for years to buy their first home, they decided they would not compromise with anything they did to the house, inside or outside. They were determined that everything would be the best quality they could afford. If they could not afford the best, they would wait and save a bit more until they had enough. As their first Christmas in the new house drew near, Ron decided it was time to put the pool in. Anyone who has had an in-ground pool put in will tell you how easily it can turn into a nightmare, but Ron and Julianne knew they would be okay because their number-one priority, as with everything else in the house, was quality. They paid a substantial deposit to a top pool company, and excavation commenced.

About three weeks later, Ron was made redundant from his job. He had only been in this job for a short time, and the payout from his previous job had all gone into the house. Ron and Julianne now had to watch every cent. The pool became a luxury they couldn't really afford, but they had paid their deposit and were committed to the pool company. Worse still, they had already sent out invitations for Christmas lunch – featuring a cartoon of Ron and Julianne in their new pool – to Julianne's entire extended family.

As the weeks passed and the bills got out of control, the pool became the proverbial nightmare. The builder said he could cut costs if he started working on another pool as well as theirs. There were many disagreements and delays, and three weeks before Christmas the pool still wasn't finished. Ron and Julianne were beside themselves with worry. They started to economise, downsizing the pool-cleaning system they had originally decided on.

After four months of arguments and sleepless nights, the pool was finally finished in March of the following year. Ron and Julianne agree that the biggest mistake they made was taking shortcuts to get it finished. They said they realise now that they should have approached their bank, let them know about Ron's situation and arranged re-financing to include the pool. Instead, they are left with something that is second-rate, which could have been avoided if they had stuck to their golden rule: *quality at all costs*.

One of my favourite sayings cuts to the chase when it comes to quality.

Quality
It's unwise to pay too much
but it's unwise to pay too little.

When you pay too much,
you lose a little money, that is all.

When you pay too little,
you sometimes lose everything,
because the thing you bought
was incapable of doing
the thing you bought it to do.

The common law of business balance
prohibits paying a little and getting a lot.

It can't be done.

If you deal with the lowest bidder,
it's well to add something for the risk you run.

And if you do that, you will have
enough to pay for something better . . .

GIVING AND RECEIVING ARE THE SAME

Have you ever thought of someone you haven't seen for ages, and then the phone rang and it was them? Or maybe you wrote a letter to that person and the next day in the mail you received a letter from them? How many times have you heard people say, 'We were just talking about you!'?

You know from previous chapters that your self-talk moves you in the direction of your current thinking, but there are no coincidences or accidents. Well, if your thinking controls the direction in which you move, what about your physical actions? How do they control what happens in your world?

You've heard the sayings, 'As you sow, so shall you reap' and 'What goes around comes around'. If you want to attract the good things in life, you must be aware that these sayings are absolutely true. I'm not talking about 'Get rich quick' schemes here – there are enough of those around from the gambling institutions. What I want to prove to you is this. If you can accept that the energy currently flowing out to the world from you is attracting whatever happens in your life, then you will feel empowered to attract whatever you want in your life from now on.

We all accept the need to breathe. We don't question it because we know if we were to stop breathing, we would die from a lack of oxygen. A wealth and abundance of anything in your life is directly related to the same thinking. If you have been given the old belief, 'Look after your cents and the dollars will look after themselves', toss it away now. It could be holding you back – here's why. Like air, you must keep the flow of money coming into and out of your life. You must keep giving to receive. It's that basic. But before you rush out and start to bowl everyone over with your generosity, take a minute to think about *why* you are giving.

Words and gestures are useless and empty if they are not given honestly. It's your *intent* that gives power to your words and gestures. When you give something to someone only to get something in return, the universe knows this and repels any success in your life. That's why working hard does not always make you successful. On the other hand, when you give with the sole intention of helping someone else, the law of the universe ensures you are rewarded.

I have experienced the power of giving in my business. For years I struggled to get it off the ground, to achieve a flow of engagements and clients that would allow me to enjoy my job and not worry about the 'wolves at the door' (the bank!).

The turnaround in my thinking came quite unexpectedly at a function on the Central Coast of New South Wales. I was presenting to a group of very successful insurance salespeople and the feeling in the room was electric. All these guys knew the power of what I was talking about, because it was what had made them successful in the first place.

At the end of the presentation, the general manager thanked me for my 'amazing talent in giving' and said that he had learned a lot. 'What did I give?' I thought to myself. Driving back to Sydney that afternoon I realised the power of what the general manager had said, and how I had changed the style of my presentations. I was no longer doing them to make money, but had let go and accepted that success would come when I threw myself 100 per cent into my job and started doing it to help people grow. While I had been trying all the time to make my presentations better in physical ways, for example, by improving my handouts and folders, the key was to change my thinking.

TRUE SECURITY

What is security? It's quite amazing how many different answers I receive when I ask this question in my talks. Here are some that were given during one seminar:

A healthy bank account

A lover to look after me

My parents

My husband/wife

My portfolio of investments

My car

My house

My job title

They are all wrong! These things do not provide security. Remember when we discussed self-esteem? We decided that no person or event can take away your self-esteem, only *you* can. You have to give permission for that person or event to take the deposits out of your Self-esteem Bank Account. You are in the pilot's seat of your life.

What, then, is security? True security comes from within. It's believing that the universe is going to look after you and keep you in the lifestyle which you have achieved. But if you think you don't deserve to live in your current lifestyle, because it is too good for you, you set out on a path of self-sabotage which will ensure that you retreat to hard times.

A case in point is Jacqui, a salesperson with a luxury-car dealership. When I conducted a seminar at her company, she came up and told me she was starting all over again for the second time. She had previously worked for another luxury-car franchise and had performed extremely well, but had let her success fall through. Instead of remaining focused, she had started to take short cuts when she dealt with customers. Where once she had received many calls a day from happy clients referring new business to her, she was reduced to taking whatever she could get from the showroom floor.

When the economy slumped as well, the importance of referral business suddenly became burningly obvious to Jacqui. All salespeople know that this is the best kind of sales work, because credibility and trust have just about been established by the previous happy customer. After many warnings to lift her game, Jacqui was laid off. She struggled for months to muster the courage to apply for her current job. With her savings just about gone and her self-esteem hitting rock-bottom, Jacqui said she had been at her lowest ebb in years.

She also said that she related to the quote, 'The teacher arrives when the student is ready' (see Chapter 10). For her, the timing of the slump in the economy and her losing her job were all part of the bigger picture, telling her to take more accountability for her performance. Jacqui learnt that, if she didn't reset her goals, she was setting herself up for failure. She knows now that if she can maintain her level of self-esteem and then build on it, her performance will only improve.

Self-sabotage is our subconscious telling us to get back to our cruising altitude, or comfort zone. Be aware of this and always on the alert for it – when you catch yourself talking yourself down, you will know it is time to re-focus on what you want, not what you don't want.

MONEY WON'T TAKE AWAY YOUR FEAR

Ask any person who has achieved greatness what they fear most. They may well say they are frightened of losing what they have. For most people, though, the biggest worries are struggling to keep the wolves from the door, or just trying to manage the household budget. These are stressful enough!

But ask most people whether they think they would have worries if they had the wealth and success of some of their favourite stars. Most of them will say that if their money worries were over, *all* their worries would be over. No way! Survey after survey documents how people who have won large sums of money get rid of much of it very quickly, because they feel so uncomfortable having a large bank balance. Another example is an actor who has waited all his life to land that role on a leading TV show. He lands the role of his dreams, then starts worrying how long the part will last. What if the ratings go down? Will he be out on his ear? Will he have to go on the dole again? This actor thought all his worries would be over once he landed that part – but they weren't.

> You are not your job.
> You are not your title.
> You are not your car.
> You are not your address.

It is your birthright to be successful, no matter what circumstances you were born into.

CHAPTER FOURTEEN

The Power of Perception

*'An ounce of image is worth
a ton of performance.'*
ANONYMOUS

IN THIS CHAPTER:

Who said people don't judge a book by its cover?
We all do!

＊

Why what you wear says a lot about who you are

＊

Dress like the person you want to become like

＊

ThinkLink and its power of connection

＊

How winners make sure they look like winners

T hink back to the last time you were driving and caught a glimpse of a sparkling BMW. What did you think about the driver? 'Loser, deadbeat'? No way. I bet you either thought: 'Wow, that guy is doing well', or you were really envious and muttered to yourself, 'Their parents must have paid for it'. If you were more comfortable with the second response, have a quick read of Chapter 13 again!

The fact is, whether you agree with it or not, 99.9 per cent of the population judges you by how you look and how you present yourself. In an address to a large Australian bank, I was asked to cover this very topic.

Tom, who had achieved middle-of-the-road success to this point, was fascinated by this issue and asked me to meet him to discuss how he could present a more professional image. The first area we targeted, and the one which could most easily be fixed, was his way of dressing. Tom had a gregarious personality and liked to wear ties that were on the 'loud' side. I asked him one question: 'If I had $50 000 to invest, possibly my life's savings, and I wanted to be reassured that you were the person I could trust to do the job, do you think a colourful Mickey Mouse tie or a classy Armani tie would be more convincing?' The answer is pretty obvious, isn't it?

DRESS LIKE THE PERSON YOU WANT TO BECOME

It's an old saying, but it's true. If you dress like the person you want to become, you start to feel different, and people will start to see you differently. Are you dressing like your next promotion?

At the very beginning of this book, you discovered that the world is a reflection of your thinking. People treat you like you want to be treated. You are telling them how you want to be treated both subconsciously and consciously. Well, the way you dress is telling everyone what you think about yourself, and how far you think you will go in the company. Every industry has its style and certain do's and don't's, so here are a few questions you might like to ask yourself or pay attention to over the next week or two. You will be amazed at what you start to notice.

Remember, the goal comes first, then we see how to get it. Start to focus on dress and presentation, and you will see some quick things you could do to improve your chances of promotion. Who is regarded as the best at the job you want? How do they dress? What do they drive?

You might have heard the saying, 'Think globally, act locally'. Well, in this case you need to do just that. Look around and see what's working (it's called 'benchmarking'), and then change it to suit you. Why reinvent the wheel?

THINKLINK

Every day I think about the line: 'An ounce of image is worth a ton of performance'. I call this concept 'ThinkLink', to describe how what you see immediately links to the way you think about it.

Robert Crandell, the chairman of American Airlines, summed this up beautifully with an example involving passengers on board. He said that the airline had noticed that passengers who had not flown frequently and were a little bit nervous, would sometimes pull down the tray table in front of them before take-off. He said that while the staff didn't know why the passengers did this, it was clear that if these passengers pulled down the tray table in front of them and saw a coffee stain, they would automatically think, 'How are they servicing the engines?! If near enough is good enough inside the plane, what's the attitude like outside the plane?'

This is a great example of how perception is reality for all of us. Who cares how things *really* are? It's how you *think* they are that counts. Engineers will tell you that when designing a bridge, one of the first conditions is to satisfy the question: does it look safe and dependable? All the

162

latest styles and designs will count for nothing if the public shy away from it because they see the bridge as unsafe.

Can you remember being at the footy and finding a hair in your hot-dog? Or what about that restaurant that has great food, but one day you saw a mouse run through it, heading towards the kitchen? Or when that used-car salesman dressed as if he just stepped out of *Saturday Night Fever* said, 'Trust me'!

You Can Tell a Good Painter by His Brushes!

One example of ThinkLink that really hits the mark was told to me by my painter, Chris. He was happily painting away and asking me about my seminars when I started to explain ThinkLink. I shared the story about the coffee stain on the tray table, and Chris said, 'It's the same with painters and tradespeople'.

I was surprised at this, and said, 'In what way?' Chris explained that, when you're trying to decide whether to employ a painter or not, the best way to tell if they take pride in their work is to ask to see their brushes.

'Their what?' I said.

'Their brushes', he replied. 'You can always tell how a paint job will turn out before the painter starts by looking at his brushes. If he can't keep his brushes clean, what else will he consider not important on the job?'

I remember when I first met Andrea, my gardener. I had phoned her in response to an advertisement she had placed in the local paper. I called and arranged for her to come and look over the lawn and garden she would have to maintain, then give me a quote.

As soon as she arrived, I knew she was going to get the job. I had made up my mind even before I spoke to her! Her van was immaculate, with a classy company logo painted on the side in a deep forest-green colour. Then, as soon as I met her, I knew this was someone who not only took pride in her work, but loved what she did. Needless to say, her work is excellent, as I knew it would be all along.

It's been said that our 'gut feeling' is always right. What gut feeling do you think people get when they see you arrive for a meeting or party? Does your style of dress tell everyone you are stuck in the 1980s, for example, or does it say that you take pride in how you present yourself?

Some people find the topic of 'image' crass and shallow – that is, until they go from job to job with no success, or their business performs so badly they sit up and take notice. They realise that everyone thinks the same way, and that perception really is reality.

CUSTOMER SERVICE

One of the most profound areas that can be affected by perception is customer service. After sharing 'ThinkLink' in my seminar, I get some amazing input on how particular organisations control perception. Here are just a few:

- The hygienic label wrapped around the toilet seat in most motels/hotels for new check-ins means: 'This has been cleaned thoroughly for you. In fact, no one has ever sat here before!'
- Food handlers wearing gloves means: 'We really care about your safety'.
- Technicians placing a plastic sheet over your car seat and a paper mat in the footwell before working on your treasured baby means: 'We care about your car. We will look after it.' (But technicians doing wheelies as they take it away means: 'Do you really trust us with your car?')
- The smell of freshly baked muffins through a house when it's up for sale and open for inspection means: 'What a warm and friendly home you're in. Just imagine the great times you will have here.'
- We have all watched those medical dramas, 'ER' and 'Chicago Hope'. What most of us have not seen in real life is all the blood that gets on those very clean, very white garments the doctors wear. How would you feel if the doctor who had just finished operating on your dear mother's heart came out still wearing a blood-soaked white coat to tell you that everything went fine? No way. The medical profession knows all about perception, so the first thing they do after washing up after an operation, is to change into a clean white garment, letting you know that they are still in their work gear, but everything went fine.

I have heard many 'war stories' about perception, both good and bad, but the ones in the following chapter are the most memorable and those that I like to share in my seminar. They all scream out that message: 'An ounce of image is worth a ton of performance'.

CHAPTER FIFTEEN

Exceeding Expectations – We All Love It!

'What goes around comes around.'

ANONYMOUS

IN THIS CHAPTER:

How a top hotel exceeded expectations

✳

How a car dealership listened, then put the boot in

✳

How a free car wash backfired

✳

How exceeding expectations can recharge a marriage

✳

Why exceeding expectations keeps customers coming back

✳

Mistakes can be the best opportunity to impress

✳

We all love surprises – any time

T he Park Hyatt Sydney has established itself as the best hotel in Australia. In the hotel business, they say that three things guarantee a hotel will be successful: location, location and location. The Park Hyatt, nestled on the water's edge underneath the Harbour Bridge and opposite the Opera House, qualifies in every sense when it comes to location. But the general manager, Willi Martin, and his team know it takes more than a great location to remain on top.

Gordon Fuller, the Park Hyatt's Executive Assistant Manager, shared this story with me to demonstrate how this hotel is always trying to exceed its guests' expectations. An American guest rang the Park Hyatt concierge and asked whether he could organise a case of oranges to be sent to her father in Chicago for his birthday. Her father was particularly fond of 'Florida' oranges, but the guest knew that this variety was not available in Australia and said she was happy for the concierge to send 'any' oranges.

After speaking to the guest, the concierge immediately telephoned a contact in Florida, who arranged to freight a box of 'Florida' oranges to the guest's father in Chicago. When she heard this, the guest was ecstatic and overwhelmed with the service provided by the team at the hotel.

Almost Heaven on Delivery

About six years ago I was at the Melbourne Motor Show, where Toyota's new luxury car, the Lexus, was to be launched. I was with a client, Adam, who, like me, is a bit of a car nut. He had heard great things about this car from his associates in the USA and was determined to invest in one here when they became available. When we approached the Toyota stand, he saw the Lexus LS400. The sticker price was about $120 000, which was a bargain compared to the BMWs and Mercedes Benzes on offer.

About three weeks later, Adam phoned me to say that he had inspected an Australian-delivered Lexus and could not believe all the gadgetry. When I asked what he liked the most he said it would have to be the six-stack CD located in the boot of the car. He explained that you could travel from Sydney to Melbourne and never have to touch a CD – all you had to do to change them was use the controls on the console. Six years ago this was big news, and he was thrilled. When he was being shown the other features of the car, the salesperson asked casually what kind of music he would look forward to playing on the CD system. He said that country and western was his favourite, especially John Denver.

About a month passed and Adam called me again. He had just taken delivery of his new Lexus. Lexus made a big deal of delivering the car, with flowers for his wife and chocolates all round. Then, when he started the engine to drive his new baby for the first time, throughout the cabin came 'Almost heaven, West Virginia . . .' Yes, John Denver was playing and 'Rocky Mountain High' wasn't the only high – Adam was ecstatic. He could not believe that, after asking what kind of music he liked a few weeks ago, the salesperson had gone to the trouble of purchasing a John Denver CD and putting it in the stacker. Unbelievable – and also very unexpected!

Service Too Good to Be True

Peter, one of Australia's leading car dealers, shared this story with me recently. He frequently travels on business around Australia and the world and has stayed at many hotels and resorts. Peter and his wife, Megan, travelled to the Sheraton Mirage on the Gold Coast for a long weekend, to escape Sydney's windy August. He had been to the hotel recently for a dealers' conference, and thought it would be ideal for a quick getaway. Peter had also heard that the Mirage's Mississippi mud cake was outstanding, and was determined to have at least one piece while dining there. On the Saturday afternoon, Peter rang Horizons restaurant in the hotel to book a table for dinner that evening. He thought he'd better make sure that mud cake was on the menu. The restaurant staff member on the phone chuckled and said yes, it was, and that she would be working that evening and would look forward to meeting Peter and his family.

At 7.30 pm, after welcoming them to the restaurant, Monica, who had taken Peter's original booking, pointed out the mud cake and showed them to their table. All was going well until 9.00 pm, when the kids started to become restless. Peter and Megan decided they would return to their room, and that dessert and the mud cake would have to wait for another time. About forty minutes later, after the kids had been put to bed, there was a knock on the door. It was Monica from the restaurant. She said that she had noticed that the kids were restless, and that they had left without having dessert. Knowing how much Peter wanted the Mississippi mud cake, she had decided to bring him and Megan a plunger with coffee for two, some port, and – you guessed it – two slices of mud cake. Complimentary, of course! Peter said he would never forget this event, ever.

LIFTING THE CROSSBAR

Adam's and Peter's stories are examples of the amazing things that happen when you lift people's expectations. What happens next? Suddenly everything has to be as good. And sometimes, the new expectation can shock everyone involved.

At a recent follow-up seminar for a Sydney car dealer, I asked everyone in the room what had happened since the seminar six weeks ago. Philip, the service manager, said he had learnt a very valuable lesson on customer expectations.

After the seminar, he had asked his staff how, as a team, they could start to improve the level of customer service in the dealership. After hearing my story about the John Denver CD in the Lexus, they decided to start washing customers' cars after every service. No ifs or buts – minor service or major service, everyone gets their car washed.

Two weeks earlier, a regular customer, Mrs Armstrong, had come into the dealership for a 20 000 km service. As they had committed to do, on completion of the service they washed Mrs Armstrong's car. She was delighted. She had been coming to the dealership for five years, and impressed already with the level of service, but the car wash really took her by surprise. Later that week, she sent a thank-you card to all the staff

171

at the service department, saying how impressed she was.

The next week, Mrs Armstrong's husband decided to bring in *his* car for a service, and, as normal, left the car for the day while he was at work. At 4.00 pm he returned to the dealership to collect his car. He went straight to the service desk, paid his account and drove away. Two days later, Philip received a phone call from Mr Armstrong saying how disappointed he was. Philip was surprised, because he thought the service had gone along without a hitch. When he asked Mr Armstrong what he was upset about, the answer shocked him: 'You guys didn't wash my car as well as my wife's car last week'!

When you decide to lift your clients' expectations of what is 'good enough', you'd better make sure that you can deliver the goods.

Flowers and Chocolates – 'But It's Not My Birthday!'

After I had shared Philip's story in one of my partner seminars, I met Alan. He took me aside and said that he had succeeded in turning around his relationship with the same thinking. When I asked him to elaborate, he said that when he was first married, everything was fine, but after a couple of years and a few disagreements, the marriage started to sour. Alan found himself looking for everything that was wrong in the relationship instead of everything that was great about it. Things started to grow out of proportion.

Then he attended my sales seminar, where he learnt that the relationship between a client and a salesperson is largely determined by how they go into the relationship and what they are expecting. He said that, although this information was aimed at salespeople, he found himself relating it to his wife and their marriage. For example, when I talked about exceeding expectations for clients, he thought to himself, 'When was the last time I exceeded expectations with Sandy? When did I last surprise her with flowers or chocolates for no reason except that I love her?'

When he returned home that night with flowers and chocolates, Sandy nearly fainted from shock. After the usual 'What do you want?' stage was over (you have to expect that after such a long time between drinks!), they started talking about how they had lost direction in their relationship and what they could do to rebuild their love and commitment.

Alan told me at the partner seminar that their relationship is now the best it has ever been: 'We still have our ups and downs like any healthy relationship does, but we can sit down and talk about problems before they get out of control.' When Alan and Sandy go to parties or social gatherings now, everyone can see that their relationship is going strong by the magic aura they give out as a couple.

Hamburgers and Fruit!

On a recent visit to one of my clients in Melbourne, I found myself in the unusual position of having made good time on the notorious South-eastern Arterial (commonly referred to as the 'South-eastern Car Park'). With thirty minutes to spare, I thought I would pay a visit to the local McDonald's store, just down the road.

You can always count on McDonald's to have clean toilets, consistent food and, most of all, the morning papers. (It staggers me when I walk into a coffee lounge anywhere in Australia and ask if they have a paper. After a look of confusion, they usually come out with: 'This is a coffee shop, mate. The newsagent is four doors up.' If the newsagent is four doors up, why isn't there a morning paper, magazines etc? Total investment: all of $3.00 a day for two papers. It's the little things that keep you coming back.)

Anyway, let's return to McDonald's. I walked into the store and was pleasantly surprised to see a tablecloth on each table, as well as a vase filled with fresh flowers. This really impressed me, because it showed that the staff at this store were really trying to exceed expectations. I went to pick up the paper, and instead of a paper stand, there were about six papers all laid out. And clean! Then the pièce de résistance . . . I walked over to order my coffee and there on the counter were three cane baskets brimming with fresh fruit. I was amazed. I had been into many McDonald's stores and all were excellent, but this one broke the mould because they really lived up to the McDonald's vision, which is 'To give each customer, every time, an experience which sets new standards in Value, Service, Cleanliness and Quality'.

Things Can Go Wrong – Even with Celebrities

Sometimes the best places can make mistakes. The following story is proof that, when you exceed expectations, you can even save a situation that has gone wrong.

During a laundry service at the Park Hyatt, a shirt belonging to a celebrity from England was damaged. The shirt could not be replaced before the guest departed the hotel, as it was an American 'Gap' shirt which is not available in Australia. The guest asked the hotel to send him a Country Road shirt instead. The concierge immediately contacted the clothing company in the USA and arranged to send a shirt of the exact same colour and size to the guest, now back home in London. Upon delivery of the shirt, the well-travelled celebrity was astounded not only by the replacement, but by the speed of replacement.

I'm sure you'll agree that the stories in this chapter show how powerful perception really is. After a company seminar I gave in Sydney one after-noon, the managing director handed me a piece of paper which he said reinforced what I had said about the importance of image in business. Have a look at the opposite page and see what you think!

EXCEEDING EXPECTATIONS AT HOME AND AT WORK

Because I basically live my life 'on stage' I was fascinated to watch a TV program a couple of years ago on comedians and what makes the successful ones successful.

Every comedian agreed on the importance of the elements of surprise and exaggeration. The performers intertwine these two things in their jokes, to give them the punch that will get the audience behind them and, hopefully, in stitches. The same concept can be used in a very powerful way at home and at work.

Our customers are important people

To keep and care for customers so that they do not want to stray, remember:

1 = 11 x 5 ...	→ On average one dissatisfied customer will tell eleven others, who will tell five others. That's a lot of negative advertising.
One negative destroys twelve positives	→ It takes twelve positive service incidents to make up for one negative incident.
Complain? – No! Come back? – No!	→ 90% of customers don't complain when they have a problem – they just don't come back!
95% will come back	→ Seven out of ten complaining customers will do business with you again if you resolve the complaint in their favour. If you resolve it on the spot, 95% will do business with you again.
Poor service? Lose 10–30% of customers	→ The average Australian company will lose 10–30% of its existing customers – mostly due to poor service. Most of these customers could have been retained.
Indifference = 60% of lost customers	→ 60% of customers who stop dealing with a particular organisation do so because of company indifference.
Quality service? Grow three times as fast as competitors	→ Organisations providing quality service grow twice as fast and pick up market share three times quicker than their competitors.
Better service = increased profit	→ Businesses with low service quality lose 2% market share a year. Those with higher service quality gain 6% market share a year and charge significantly higher prices.

Without customers, there is no company.

In one of my seminars, a successful businessman told me that the key to keeping his self-esteem intact was constantly to exceed the expectations of the people with whom he comes into contact every day. He said that when he exceeds someone's expectations or surprises them with a present or some good news, they get a lift in their day – and then, as we have learnt in earlier chapters, what goes around comes around.

Each day, find someone to surprise.

It's a simple goal, really. Imagine what would happen if you made a commitment to exceed expectations once a day. Just one person a day – yes, just one! What would happen to your self-esteem? How much better would your relationships be?

How would your partner feel if you, like Alan, arrived home with flowers and chocolates after a normal day at the office? Not on your wedding anniversary, or their birthday – just because they are special. How would your kids feel if, on a Saturday afternoon during the school term, out of the blue, you said, 'We're going to the movies'? Who in your household cleans the bathroom? Or irons the clothes? What would happen if you gave them a chore-free week – no housework for a week!

What about at work? How much do you exceed expectations at work? When was the last time you delivered those figures to the accounts department one hour *before* the deadline, instead of them always having to hassle you for them? The best team players in any organisation are the ones who can not only perform their own tasks well, but get the support of their colleagues too. And the reason they can get this support? In the past, *they* have given support to others when it was needed.

Giving Great Service at the Restaurant

You saw earlier how, when you exceed expectations, people come back for more. But what happens when you, in your turn, acknowledge the people who give you great service?

I remember once reading in a hotel magazine that customers who acknowledge their service provider, such as a waiter, doorperson or flight attendant, automatically receive 50 per cent better service than if they just say the usual 'Please' and 'Thank you'. We all love to be recognised and acknowledged, and people who realise this very powerful fact always tend to be given the very best service.

Give it a go next time you're eating out. Look at your waiter's name badge and start to use their name from that moment on. And watch the fabulous service flow back to you!

What goes around comes around.

CHAPTER SIXTEEN

Balance and Feedback

'Only a mediocre person is always
at their best.'

W. Somerset Maugham

IN THIS CHAPTER:

How motivation is connected to goals

✳

When you reach your goals, you plateau out

✳

How to put the spark back into your relationship

✳

Why you run out of energy after work,
and how to get more

✳

How to reset your goals and increase your motivation

✳

Proactive feedback or reactive feedback:
which do you use?

✳

Feedback exercise to help you refocus

✳

How daily goals maintain the momentum

O ne of the most rewarding parts of my job as a speaker is that
I feel I can make a real difference to people's lives. 'Plateauing
Out' is one of the most popular parts of my seminar, because it
allows everyone to understand that they never have to go through a period
of being lost, unfocused or unhappy.

So what is Plateauing Out all about? It's very simple: when you reach
your goals in life, no matter in which area, you plateau out. To avoid this,
you need to reset your goals just before you reach them.

RESET YOUR GOALS FOR NEW-FOUND MOTIVATION

In one of my recent seminars in Sydney, I was presenting to a very successful group of businesspeople and their partners. Every one of them had
been invited to the conference because they had achieved big results in
their particular area of expertise in the corporation. About two hours into
the seminar, when I was presenting my information on Plateauing Out,
I noticed one of the couples down at the back of the room having a bit of
a giggle. At the next break, I couldn't resist. I went up and asked them what
they were laughing at. They told me the following story.

Patrick and Pamela had been married for ten years, and everything had
been fine up to about two years before they attended my seminar. Patrick
said that they had witnessed many of their friends' marriages collapse and
were feeling quite chuffed that they had withstood all the rough parts of
their years together. But things had started to go wrong all of a sudden.

First it was the little things, and then before they knew it, they were talking about separation.

What they had realised during the seminar was that they had set very specific goals during their engagement, and when they walked up the aisle, they knew exactly what they were going to strive for: a house, two kids, a trip to Hawaii and last but not least, a BMW that they had both dreamed of owning since they met. And guess what happened? Two years before the seminar they had achieved all their goals – done, finished. Success, and then – plateauing out.

Patrick said that the most amazing thing they realised by all this was that they had not seen it coming. They could see that they were becoming less enthused about their marriage and life in general, that they were becoming more negative, and that they were not as motivated to achieve things as they had once been. What was wrong? Were they losing the love for each other that they thought would last forever? Was the flame going out?

Well, nearly! After the seminar Patrick and Pamela did something pretty unusual for a couple who have been married for ten years. They took a week off and headed straight for their favourite resort island in the Whitsundays, on the Great Barrier Reef. This was where they had first planned what they would do when they got married – what they wanted to achieve together – and where they had honeymooned. They thought it was appropriate that they return there to plan the next stage of their marriage, with as much precision and detail as they had ten years before.

Where is your relationship going? Is it stale and needing a good push along? Take time now to discuss together what you both want to achieve. For Patrick and Pamela, planning and discussion put their marriage back on track and gave them a new-found sense of purpose and desire for each other.

One afternoon recently, Patrick phoned me to say that Pamela was expecting their third child and that it was all due to me. I knew what he meant – I think! Patrick continued, saying he wondered how many of their friends' marriages could have been saved if they had done what he and Pamela had done – instead of concentrating on what was wrong with their relationship, they became more focused on what was going well and where they wanted to go from then on.

TIRED AFTER WORK?

Have you ever arrived home from work, exhausted? How did you feel? I bet you just wanted to sit in front of the TV and relax. And then, after a bit of channel surfing, you found yourself snoozing.

But some nights after work, you have plans. You are invited to dinner at a friend's place, or maybe some relatives are flying in from interstate and have asked you to meet them in the city for dinner and a show. What happens? You find yourself looking forward to the dinner, and on an evening when you would normally fall asleep, you stay wide awake and instead of 'flopping', you excitedly get ready. Can you see the difference? One night you're bored and tired and suddenly the next night you're full of energy.

Why the change? Well, on one of the nights, you set a goal. Look at the energy it created. Look at the excitement you felt. All from deciding what you wanted.

GET A LIFE!

During a recent conference attended by 200 people, I asked: 'Who has spent a full day in the last six months either in a national park or on the beach?' Only three hands went up! Can you believe that? When I asked the question, I expected at least fifteen hands. (To be fair, I did ask this question in the middle of winter, but still, that's when I believe our national parks are at their best. And compared to Hawaii and Bali, our beaches are immaculate and empty during the winter.) I am making a big deal about this because I really believe that planning the occasional special weekend has kept me sane during a schedule that finds me in every capital city every month, every year.

High achievers know that if they are to constantly keep up the pace, they have to relax. Entertainers have a saying: 'You are only as good as your last performance'. But I don't think this applies only to entertainers.

I receive speaking engagements up to one year in advance. Sometimes, it's a matter of only two weeks in advance. I have noticed that when I am constantly looking forward, I remain on top of things and feel good. As soon as I start to reflect on what I have achieved, a malaise sets in, and I become complacent and bored.

On a daily level I see this in an even more obvious way. When I speak on a Thursday, and know that my next engagement is not until the following Monday, I suddenly go into 'long-weekend mode'. Long-weekend mode is when I shut down and start to unwind. But if I'm speaking on a Thursday and know I am speaking on the Friday or Saturday as well, I stay pumped up and ready to go. In other words, without an immediate goal to focus on, I plateau out.

Have a look at how much planning you are putting into your weekends. This is super-important, because how you feel when you return to work after your weekend will affect how you perform that week. Think back to a time when you were looking forward to a really exciting event that was planned way ahead. Maybe it was a good friend's wedding or twenty-first birthday party, or a school reunion. Remember how for weeks you kept on finding yourself looking forward to the day? It kept you motivated during the busiest times.

Writing this book has been a lesson in motivation for me. Anyone who has written a book will tell you it is a huge task. For me, the most fascinating part has been that I have actually done it. My speaking engagements have increased, my consulting work continues to grow at a hectic rate, and yet I still found enough hours in my life to write. In Chapter 4 I talked about setting deadlines, and that a goal without a deadline will always remain a dream. I could have had many valid excuses to delay publication of my book, but once I agreed on the deadline for material with Penguin, I surprised myself with the amount of vigour and energy I could muster.

In Chapter 4 I also said that once you set your goal, everything from then on either pulls you towards your goal or pulls you away from it. I found that as soon as the deadline was agreed and the publication date set in place, I was always asking myself, 'Is this the most productive use of my time, or could I be working on the book?' There is no way I would have self-talked like this if I did not have a goal to move towards.

What else could you squeeze into your life if you had to? Where have you plateaued out? Where have you not reset your goals to spark that new burst of energy? Take a little time now to reset your goals, and watch the motivation flow.

PROACTIVE OR REACTIVE?

Think about the last time you went to the dentist. What motivated you to go? It was probably one of two things: either you received a check-up reminder note in the mail, or you were in so much pain that the thought of hearing that rotten noise the drill makes was overtaken by the desire to get rid of the pain.

Well, in a way, we all make this kind of choice daily. Thankfully we don't have to go to the dentist every day, but in other areas of our life, we are faced with the same dilemma: to act *before* things go bad, or to try to fix them after they have already collapsed.

For example, doctors have been telling us for decades now that a low-fat diet will help prevent heart attacks. But some of us have the heart attack, and *then* change our diet. Of course, once you have had the heart attack, the damage is done. Similarly, you can obtain feedback *before* your relationship turns sour – or you can wait for it to fall apart, then try to rescue it. As with the dentist example, how much pain do you want to go through before you act?

Feedback Is the Breakfast of Champions
The diagram on the next page is very easy to fill in, but it takes two things: honesty and time. We all have huge demands on our time, but it *is* possible to fit in everything you want to do. I hear you saying, 'Oh yeah? I have five kids to look after!' or 'You don't know what it's like doing shift work'.

But saying these things doesn't achieve anything. The reality is that every person I have ever met finds time management a challenge. No one is immune. The only difference between those who succeed with it and those who don't is that the winners know that they are the only one who can fix their problems. Total accountability – no ifs or buts.

The circle below is an excellent start towards working out how to manage your time better. I use it every Sunday night. By simply filling in the large white circle according to how my life went the previous week, I can work out what I want to change in the coming week and fill in the outer grey circle accordingly. Doing this means I can steer my life in the direction I want it to go, and not be tossed about by unexpected events.

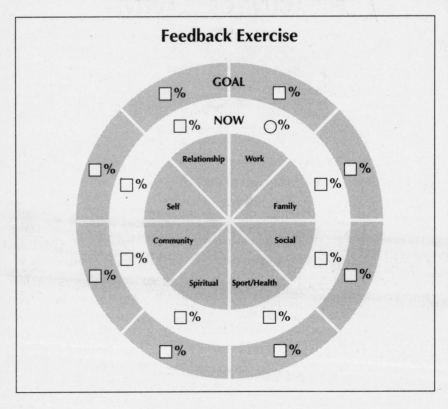

Feedback Exercise

Fill in the large white circle first ('NOW') – it represents how you feel you are currently living your life. Start with the 'Work' segment, where you will see a small circle. In this circle put a figure that you think represents how much time you have spent at work in the last two to three weeks. Then complete the rest of the 'NOW' circle, remembering not to exceed 100 per cent, and counting only your waking hours.

Next, work on the outer grey circle, which represents how you would like to see your life. Fill in the small squares with figures, adding up to 100 per cent. You can fill in the circle for the coming week, or use it in a broader, 'life' perspective.

Are there any surprises? Most people who fill out this diagram at a seminar say it makes them realise how little time they have for themselves or their family. As the business world gets more competitive, everyone is under pressure to work longer hours. If you don't change the way you plan your personal life, you might find that it disappears. Just like in goal-setting, whatever you don't focus on ends up being screened out of your life. You stop noticing opportunities to spend more time with your partner or kids, and before you know it, they're not there any more. The kids have grown up and have more important things to do than watch TV with mum and dad.

Just think about the planning you would do if you were travelling overseas for a few weeks. It's pretty unlikely that you would just turn up at an international airport, pick a country, pick an airline, board and then take off. All of these decisions must be made before you embark on the journey. What's the difference with life? Nothing. Have a destination for the week and map out some of the stops along the way, and watch how smooth your week becomes. Time will just 'appear'!

I Want Time with My Twin Boys

One of the 3000 Qantas employees who have been to my seminar was an excellent case in point regarding time management.

Luigi is the son of Italian immigrants who came to Australia when he was a toddler. He had been promoted to supervisor six months before the seminar, and was working long hours. He didn't want to let the opportunity of this job pass as he felt it was his big chance at success. Luigi's problem was that, while he had no problem putting in the time at work, he was seeing less and less of his young twin boys, Marco and Gino. At the seminar he asked me what I thought he could do to find more time to spend with his sons.

After filling in the white circle in the exercise above, Luigi made a commitment to spend more time with his boys, no matter what. He said, 'Before I know it, I'll be throwing them their eighteenth birthday party! Life is too short for that.'

A month passed and I saw Luigi again while I was waiting for a meeting with a senior executive. He said the most amazing thing had happened two weeks before. He was watching the news after finishing work and was hit by what felt like a bolt of lightning. Marco yelled out, 'Dad, we're off to soccer', which meant the kids were going next door to get a lift with their neighbour, Mrs Jones, whose son also played soccer. Mrs Jones had been driving the boys to soccer practice every Tuesday and Thursday night for about three years.

Luigi said that as soon as Marco had said, 'Bye, dad', the lightning hit him. *He* should be taking his sons to soccer practice! That way he would have at least another two hours with them every week. Then and there he spoke to Mrs Jones and arranged to alternate the driving with her.

When you decide you want more time for something, and that nothing is going to stop you, it's amazing what will show itself to you. The goal or end result must come first – then you will see how to achieve it.

You Get Instant Feedback at Work

I will never forget what happened at a workshop I gave at a conference about two years ago. I was at the point in the seminar where I talk about 'feedback', emphasising how much you need it at home as well as at work.

I said, 'How many of you think you might be a bit off course at home?' Frank, who was sitting towards the front, said, 'Look, mate, I don't have any problems at home. All my problems and stress are caused by this damn place [his workplace].' One of his colleagues, Craig, chimed in with, 'That's because your kids can't resign – they're stuck with you.'

There was a moment of silence in the room. Everyone knew what Craig was talking about. We get heaps of feedback at work if we veer even the slightest bit off course, but at home we usually wait for the problem to cause us a lot of pain before we recognise it and take steps to fix it.

The Balance Is Never Right

Another interesting point to note about the feedback sheet is this: without exception, every successful person who has attended my program is surprised to notice after filling it in that they have let a few things in life slip through. They see themselves as very focused, but with the constant barrage of change in their life, they realise they may have been spending too much time on the golf course with clients instead of having a picnic lunch with their partner. Or they may have been slacking off at work and taking long lunches a bit too often.

188

They are not the ones who sit there and come back with, 'Yeah, things are going great'. The successful ones know they need to be resetting their goals all the time. They realise that if they don't take a good look at themselves and how their life is going, they could find themselves plateauing out.

Amanda, a successful accountant, was a good example. She realised that the reason she was not getting on very well with her adolescent kids was because she had not adjusted her work regime to fit in time for them during this challenging and difficult period for them. Instead of getting angry when her son, Brett, said he didn't want to come to grandma's for lunch, Amanda realised it was okay for Brett to stay home and watch a video or play on his computer. Her son was just trying to create his own life and make his own decisions.

Amanda knew that if she kept on nagging Brett, it would only cause pain for both of them. At this vulnerable time in their lives, teenagers need to know that they are worthwhile, and that their parents are friends who are on their side. Amanda said, 'It's just dawned on me – hit me like a ton of bricks.' What she had realised was that everything in Brett's life must be in a state of flux. He is changing physically, mentally and sexually and must be wondering what is happening to him.

'And I'm nagging him to go to his grandma's! He needs a friend, and I have not been that person. I'm still the mother that was okay five years ago when he was eight years old. But now he wants some freedom, and if I don't let him have it, I can see that he'll go the way of one of my brother's kids who felt so constrained he hit out and got into trouble with the police. I guess I was so caught up with the changes at work that I couldn't see the enormous change happening right in front of me at home.'

THE DAILY GOALS PLANNING SHEET

The following sheet is one of the most popular in my seminar. Most people recognise it from one that their corporation already has, but many fail to see the power of using it on a daily basis.

Before you finish work for the day, whatever it is – in an office, on the road, or at home with the kids – write down what you want to achieve the

YOU CAN DO IT!

Daily Goals

Things I will do today

Day:_____ Date:_____

PRIORITY	TASK	COMPLETED
❑	1._____	❑
❑	2._____	❑
❑	3._____	❑
❑	4._____	❑
❑	5._____	❑
❑	6._____	❑
❑	7._____	❑
❑	8._____	❑
❑	9._____	❑
❑	10._____	❑
❑	11._____	❑
❑	12._____	❑
❑	13._____	❑
❑	14._____	❑
❑	15._____	❑
❑	16._____	❑
❑	17._____	❑
❑	18._____	❑
❑	19._____	❑
❑	20._____	❑

following day. The list doesn't have to be in any order: just put down things as they come to mind.

When you have listed everything you can think of, go down the left-hand side of the page and prioritise, in order of importance. Mark the most important tasks, to be done as soon as you get to work, with an 'A'. Mark the second most important tasks with a 'B'. The things you will do when the As and Bs are done are marked with a 'C'.

Improved Focus

Can you imagine how focused you will become when you start to make a list of things to do every night?

Remember in Chapter 4 you discovered how, when you are focused on something, you start to see how to achieve it? This is what will happen when you write down your goals for the following day. You will start to see things that previously were right in front of you, but because you didn't know you needed them, your lack of focus caused you not to notice them.

Similarly, I gave examples in Chapter 3 of shopping for a birthday present and choosing a video. When you knew exactly what you wanted it jumped off the shelf, yet when you went to the shop with no ideas, you returned home with nothing.

The same analogy applies with your daily goals. The people who consistently get through the most in a day are the ones who are focused on what they want, who have thought about their goals for that day. When they arrive at work, they are so focused that anything to do with their goals is right there in front of them.

Turn Off When You Leave
and Start Up Again with a Bang!

The most fascinating aspect of the Daily Goals Planning Sheet is that when you write everything down, it seems that your conscious mind sends everything to your subconscious. So later, when you're playing tennis or having dinner with your family, your mind will be on the task at hand, i.e. tennis or dinner, not on work.

Why? Well, when you have written down what you need to accomplish, your conscious mind can focus on other things and start to relax about work, because it knows everything has been recorded.

The next morning, see what happens. For many people, focus at work only begins after the second cup of coffee. But if you use the Daily Goals Planning Sheet, you will find mornings a lot easier. All you really have to do is plan a bit better and bingo! Your motivation will start to lift.

'The Boss Never Thanks Me'

I can't remember how many times I have heard this comment! I think many people in my seminar are a bit surprised when I tell them they won't be getting any thanks from the boss in the future, either. That feedback comes from yourself, not your boss. Imagine if you were going really well at work. Would you be whingeing, 'Why doesn't the boss thank me?' No way! When you know you're going well, you don't need others to confirm it. You convince yourself.

When you have accomplished fifteen of the eighteen tasks you set yourself yesterday on your Daily Goals Planning Sheet, how do you think you will feel? Your self-talk will be saying, 'I'm on a roll. Things are really coming together. I'm really getting things done!' You will be taking total accountability for your performance and self-esteem – not leaving it to chance.

Your life is too important to leave it to chance. Remember those famous words from the hit movie, *Dead Poets Society*? *Carpe diem* – seize the day!

WANT TO KNOW MORE ABOUT . . . ?

CHAPTER SEVENTEEN

Seeing Greatness in Others

'If you would win a man to your cause,
first convince him that you are
his sincere friend.'

ABRAHAM LINCOLN

IN THIS CHAPTER:

The Pygmalion Concept, or how to make winners

✳

How the Boomerang Concept can change
people's performance

✳

From 'dumb class' to 'top achievers'

✳

Partners as Pygmalions

✳

Why 'stirring' is no laughing matter

✳

Your kids are awesome!

✳

How kids learn from adults

You can't get much more Australian than the boomerang. Recently, I was guest speaker at a conference at Uluru, or Ayers Rock. As you probably know, the Red Centre is a must-see stop on any overseas visitor's agenda, so it was no surprise to see a fabulous collection of native art for sale at the visitors' centre. On the top of the list for tourists is the boomerang, not only because of the brilliant artwork that adorns it, but because of the mystery of how such a simply shaped object can perform so incredibly.

Well, the Boomerang Concept is pretty much the same. Just by having a simple belief about someone, you can lift their performance to incredible heights, or destroy them.

THE BOOMERANG CONCEPT

The 'Boomerang Concept', or the 'Pygmalion Concept' as it is also known, comes from Greek mythology. Pygmalion was a sculptor who loved sculpting statues, which he usually then sold. However, he decided he would like to keep one creation, a beautiful maiden. The myth has it that one of the gods fired the arrow of belief into Pygmalion's new statue, and suddenly she came to life. Thus, the 'Pygmalion Concept' has come to mean that if you believe in someone enough, you can make them achieve anything.

Those of you who are old enough will remember the musical *My Fair Lady*, which is based on the play *Pygmalion* by George Bernard Shaw. In the musical, Eliza Doolittle is transformed from a lowly flower seller to a 'lady' because, as she says in the movie, 'Professor 'Enry 'Iggins *saw* me as a lady.'

And then there's *My Fair Lady II*. Oh sorry, I meant *Pretty Woman*! It has the same theme as *My Fair Lady*, but instead of a professor and a flower seller, it's a millionaire and a prostitute (a bit more 1990s, wouldn't you agree?).

However, the theme is the same. When you believe in someone and keep on telling them they are awesome, they start to believe it.

The Dumb Class Doesn't Know It's Dumb

Many years ago, in the USA, an experiment was carried out to determine if the 'Boomerang Concept' really does work.

The setting was a school. Before the start of a new school year, the researcher laid some groundwork. He asked the principal which class was considered to be (in politically correct language) 'educationally chal-lenged', or (in plain English) 'dumb'. The principal directed him to the 'Red' class, where the students were consistently at the bottom of the form and generally regarded in the school as 'losers'. That year they were to have a new teacher. The principal and the researcher agreed not to tell this teacher that the class she had inherited was regarded as the dumbest in the school. The idea was that the researcher would hopefully be able to demonstrate that when we don't have fixed beliefs about people, they can achieve anything – if they are properly supported.

The new teacher didn't have a clue about her class. When the researcher asked her what she thought of her new pupils and how they would go that year, she replied that, as with all her students, she would endeavour to bring out the best in them, but essentially, it was up to them to achieve good results. The researcher asked if he could visit the class on two more occasions during the year – six months later, and again at the end of the year – to see how the students had gone.

Six months to the day, the researcher returned to the school and was amazed to find that most students in the 'Red' class were performing above average. At the end of the year, to his further surprise, the class was at the top of the form. He noted that as well as better grades, there was a large improvement in the students' self-esteem, evident in how they were all pre-senting themselves.

The principal was also astounded and asked the teacher what she had done to achieve such outstanding results. She was flattered but said this was her normal result with pupils, and that she did not see what all the fuss was about. She then asked why everyone was so surprised. The principal told her that she had spent the last twelve months with what was previously regarded as the worst class in the school, tagged 'the losers'.

The principal was intrigued that the teacher had not picked up any signals from the students that they were slower than others, or more restless, as is usually the case with students struggling with their work. The teacher replied that she *had* noticed a few things that were different, but was under the impression that the students were among the best in the school and just ignored the differences as 'creativity'. She went on to say that the biggest influence on why she had assumed the students were going to perform well was the IQ figures the principal had handed her at the start of the year.

'What IQ figures?' the principal asked in a surprised voice.

'The figures on the green sheet you gave me,' replied the teacher.

The principal exclaimed in amazement: 'That wasn't their IQ figures – it was their locker numbers!'

I have heard many variations on this story, but the theme remains consistent: believe in people, and they will deliver. Think back to the story of Karen and her son, Jason, in Chapter 2. Remember how Karen noticed the improvement in Jason's behaviour as soon as his self-esteem lifted? Instead of treating him like a little brat, which was how he was acting, she decided to start to see him in a better light and then, bingo – Jason's performance turned around.

I have seen the Boomerang Concept alive and well in many, many companies in Australia. The most obvious example was when one of my clients, Jeff, decided to make some organisational changes and asked me whether I thought one of his managers, Gary, had what it takes to be a general manager. My reply surprised him: 'What do *you* think?' He said that he knew Gary had all the skills needed for the job, but that he doubted Gary's ability to handle the stress that went with it. Jeff knew what I was hinting at. He knew that if *he* believed in his general manager and gave him the necessary support, Gary would come through.

'It's that "kids in the classroom" story that you share in your seminar, isn't it?' he exclaimed. 'If I really commit totally to him he will come through, just like the kids did in that classroom'. Jeff had got my point: our belief in other people is a very powerful tool that can transform them into champions.

PARTNERS ARE PYGMALIONS

Stop for a moment and think about your relationship with your partner. Are you constantly pulling them down, or are you always trying to convince them that they can achieve whatever they want?

I am always amazed at the difference between newly engaged couples and couples who have been together for ten years. These differences really seem to stand out when you're at a party. You'll see a newly engaged couple who are excited and looking forward to a long and happy future together, while the couple who have been together for ten years might not say a single word to each other after they arrive. He'll talk to his mates outside around the barbecue, and she'll stay inside and talk to the girls.

Brendan and his partner of twelve years, Rebecca, attended a seminar put on by the company Brendan worked for. They came along hoping for a little help in refocusing themselves, but Brendan told me later that the biggest eye-opener for both of them was realising how he and Rebecca constantly pulled each other down.

Brendan said that compared to the relationships he sees at parties and other functions, his relationship with Rebecca was pretty good. 'But we *had* noticed that we were starting to slip a little bit. When we were first engaged to be married, we were always complimenting each other on little things, like what the other was wearing, for example, perfume or clothes, and usually tried to motivate each other every morning before work.' But as their relationship approached the eight-to-nine-year mark, they had begun to plateau out in their personal and relationship goals, and were generally feeling less enthusiastic about going out to parties or the movies.

What made things harder for both of them was that they were trying to start a family, and they were not having any success. All their friends were having their second and third kids, and their whole social scene was based around this.

Brendan said that he and Rebecca received a good kick in the pants at the seminar: 'You delivered the material with great empathy, but the impact really hit us when you got to that part of the seminar. We really haven't been positive Pygmalions to each other. We've both been feeling sorry for ourselves instead of trying to motivate the other person.

'When it comes to giving feedback, we used to try to tell the other person something negative – say we didn't like the way the other was dressed or had their hair – without hurting their feelings. In fact, instead of criticising what they were wearing, we had a line that went like this: "I wish you'd wear that sexy black dress, the one you bought on the Gold Coast when we were on holidays." This would always bring a smile and was a nice way of saying "What you're wearing doesn't suit you." But these days, we're more likely to say straight out, "That's disgusting! Haven't you got anything better to wear?" '

The Subconscious Can't Take a Joke

Brendan said that one of my lines in particular had really hit home: 'When you said there was no such thing as a "stirrer", just a person with low self-esteem, Rebecca looked at me. She knows I am always cutting people down and then using the line, "Only kidding".'

I was intrigued to hear the saying, 'The subconscious can't take a joke'. When you make fun of other people, even though you are joking, they can get hurt. That's why flight simulators can be used so effectively, because your subconscious can't tell the difference between a real and an imagined event. For the same reason, rehearsing and visualising your goals works. If you imagine something often enough, it will happen.

It's the same with relationships. If you are constantly telling someone that they are 'useless' or that they have 'lost it', they will eventually start to believe it.

'MY KIDS ARE AWESOME – I JUST COULDN'T SEE IT'

As a speaker, I look forward to hearing which part of my presentation the audience has enjoyed the most. But nothing prepared me for what I heard at the end of a seminar in Melbourne one Christmas. The organisation had invited partners to attend the seminar, so I was speaking to a whole cross-section of people and ages. I finished the seminar, and as is customary, I made my way outside the room to chat to the audience on an informal basis. I find that everyone loves to share a story on how they related to my presentation, and I love to listen.

About five minutes in, a big ex-footballer-type approached me. He asked if he could have a minute when I was free. I said, 'No problem', and as soon as I had finished speaking with the current person, I approached this big fellow. Max said that he was pretty shaken up by my presentation. When I asked why, he elaborated: 'When you shared the story about the teacher and the kids who were expected not to do well, I thought of my own kids. I realised as you were talking that the reason my kids are not going so well is because I keep bagging them and telling them they will never get anywhere.' At this stage, he started to get upset. I asked him if he would like to meet me for coffee after lunch, when the rest of the group had returned to work. He was grateful and agreed to meet me at 2.00 pm.

This is the very best part of what I do as a speaker. If I can assist just one person to achieve something, then each presentation is a success. When we met later, Max apologised for getting upset before. I said, 'Don't be crazy. You have just discovered a major gift in yourself, and you are now able to go out there and share it with the world.'

Max continued: 'Not only have I been bagging my kids, but my wife has just about had enough of me nagging her and seeing the negative angle to everything that happens. What I am really glad about is that I feel I can now change and start to motivate my kids and Janet to achieve bigger things.'

When I asked Max whether he had got anything out of the seminar to help him personally, he said: 'You kept on saying during the presentation that "We can't give away something we don't have", so I will be working on lifting my Self-esteem Bank Balance. Your comment from the Chinese that "Running water flows downhill" also struck a chord with me. I really am going to try and be the "inspiration person" around the home instead of "Mr Negative" like I have been.'

A few weeks later I received a letter from Max. He said that the past two months were 'the most relaxing and enjoyable of his marriage to date'. He had started to search for ways in which he could find 'greatness' in his kids and his wife, and as a consequence, the love that has flowed back to him from them has been tremendous. But the most unexpected flow-on has been at his workplace. He said that everyone, from the boss down, had noticed his new, upbeat nature and the turnaround in his attitude – not only to his job, but to his colleagues.

Attached to Max's letter was a copy of 'Children Learn What They Live'. He said he found this after my seminar and it really hit home.

Children Learn What They Live

If a child lives with criticism,
It learns to condemn.
If a child lives with hostility,
It learns to fight.

If a child lives with ridicule,
It learns to be shy.
If a child lives with shame,
It learns to be guilty.

If a child lives with tolerance,
It learns to be patient.
If a child lives with encouragement,
It learns confidence.

If a child lives with praise,
It learns to appreciate.
If a child lives with fairness,
It learns justice.

If a child lives with security,
It learns to have faith.
If a child lives with approval,
It learns to like itself.

If a child lives with acceptance and friendship,
It learns to find love in the world.

Dorothy Law Nolte

WANT TO KNOW MORE ABOUT ... ?

Closing Remarks

In a world that is changing so fast and constantly bombarding you with information, there is one thing you still have control of – your thoughts. No one can tell you how to think about anything. You, and only you, control how you evaluate events and where they will take you.

But like everything in life, it's ACTION that counts. As you have seen throughout *You Can Do It!*, no one can change you. Only *you* can change you. You must *want* to change, and for that to happen, your initial desire has to be built upon.

You wouldn't dream of planting a seed in the garden and then expect to see a fully grown shrub or flower the next day, would you? It takes time. If a seed has the right soil and light and is watered regularly, it will grow and eventually show the effort that has been put in by displaying a beautiful flower. Why should it be any different for something you are trying to 'grow' in yourself? If you plant the right seeds (your goals) and constantly nourish them (maintain your self-esteem), then in time you will see the results of your hard work. Of course, if the seed is planted but not nourished, you can't really hope to see a flower. We all need goals to strive for and nourishment to stay on top of things.

Over the last decade I have seen this principle in action in companies throughout Australia – for instance where a manager suddenly finds he has a star employee on his hands because he decided to provide positive feedback instead of constant criticism. I have seen it when couples who have been to my seminar tell me how much they are enjoying being together now they are focused on goals that both of them want to achieve. And nothing quite stops me in my tracks like the moments when a teenager, after hearing about goal-setting and self-esteem for the first time, comes up to me at the end of a seminar and says 'That was really cool!'

When you picked up this book, you had something you wanted to achieve. I sincerely hope that I have been able to give you some ideas to help you get to wherever you want to go.

In closing, I would like to share the words of the great Winston Churchill, who said:

NEVER GIVE IN
NEVER
NEVER
NEVER
NEVER

Suggested Further Reading

The following books have really had an impact in my life. They inspired me when I started to doubt myself, or assisted me when I was challenged by events – at home and at work. Choose just one from the list, and I know you will benefit, as I have, from the writer's ability and examples.

Blanchard, Ken & Johnson, Spencer. *The One Minute Manager.* Candle Communications, 1981.

Covey, Stephen. *The 7 Habits of Highly Effective People.* The Business Library, 1990.

Gawain, Shakti. *Creative Visualisation.* Bantam Books, 1986.

Gray, John. *Men Are From Mars, Women Are From Venus.* HarperCollins, 1993.

Hay, Louise L. *You Can Heal Your Life.* Specialist Publications, 1984.

Hill, Napoleon. *Think and Grow Rich.* Hawthorn Books, 1937.

Jeffers, Susan. *Dare to Connect.* Random House, 1992.

Lindbergh, Anne Morrow. *Gift from the Sea.* Chatto & Windus, 1955.

Maltz, Maxwell. *Psycho Cybernetics.* Prentice Hall, 1960.

Peck, M. Scott. *The Road Less Travelled.* Arrow Books, 1978.

Schwartz, David J. *The Magic of Thinking Big.* Fireside Books, 1959.

Sun Tzu. *The Art of War.* Shambhala, 1991.

Wilson, Paul. *Instant Calm.* Penguin Books, 1995.

Acknowledgements

I am writing these acknowledgements overlooking the panorama of Sydney's beautiful Pittwater. In the distance sits famous Lion Island, with its charismatic and calming stance. In the foreground are hundreds of white yachts, which seem, by their position and poise, to have come to worship the lion.

The vista before me is complete not just because of Lion Island, but because of each and every yacht that goes to make up the total picture. They are all vital, and writing a book is no different. While my name appears on the front cover, making a vista like *You Can Do It!* come together has involved the commitment and dedication of many people behind the scenes.

JULIE GIBBS, the publisher at Penguin Books who saw the potential of *You Can Do It!* in our first meeting and whose belief and commitment have not wavered one inch. She is the total professional. Thank you, Julie.

KATIE PURVIS, my editor and genius at Penguin who took a speaker and made him an author. Thanks for your patience and absolute dedication, Katie.

HARRY M. MILLER, my agent and the king of deal-making. He has taught me the power of connections. You're reading one!

PETER RITCHIE, CHARLIE BELL, GUY RUSSO, RON MUSSALLI, MICHAEL NICHOLAS and all the dynamic team at McDonald's Australia. I still pinch myself that I have had the pleasure to work with over 3000 McDonald's people. A more focused group of people you will never find.

DICK SIMPSON, whom I call Mr Optus and Mr Optimist. His attitude proves you can enjoy business and make the tough calls at the same time. He has taught me the power of humour.

PETER CAPP, who is one of my recent clients, but what an impact. Cappy leads from the front, and has taught me the power of making people totally accountable. What a dynamo!

BROOKE TABBERER, who always believed that I could deliver the goods. Her commitment to me in the early days of my speaking career was outstanding. Brooke demonstrated every day the power of Win Win!

KEN TAGG, with whom I could relate so well. While Ken has achieved enormous success as Australia's largest McDonald's franchisee, he still retains the down-to-earth personality I admire so much. He has taught me humility.

KEN WRIGHT, whose passionate belief in his people is mind-boggling. He doesn't only use words to motivate them – more importantly, his actions are very powerful. He has taught me the power of creating focused teams.

NEIL SUTTON, who, over a few beers on his boat, taught me more about business than most people learn at university in a lifetime. A great storyteller who can bring the basics of business to life without the crap.

HOWARD DAVY, whom I met as a client seven years ago, and now count as one of my closest confidants in business. His uncanny ability to make people feel at ease is a true gift.

My mum, ANN HANNA, who found herself a widow at forty-four, with six kids and a business, but got right in there and did it. Her tenacity and resilience are unbelievable. I love you so much, mum.

MARY HANNA, my kid sister who, when the chips were down in the lean times, showed vision and strength beyond her years. I will never forget it, Mary.

My brothers, GEORGE and JOSEPH, and sisters, MARGARET and GERADINE, who have supported me on this amazing journey called life. We have shared the good and the bad times.

ALL MY CLIENTS over nearly a decade. Thank you for your support and commitment. I have loved sharing my material with you.

EACH PERSON who has shared the stories that make up the case studies in *You Can Do It!* While I have changed the names, you know who you are and I thank you for your generosity.

Finally, to Willi Martin and all the staff at THE PARK HYATT, SYDNEY. From day one you have spoilt me. Every time I arrive it's like coming home. Thanks, guys!

If you would like to find out more details about my other books and tapes, why not visit my web site at www.paulhanna.com? There is also a facility on the web site where you can send me email. I look forward to hearing from you.

In his no-hype, down-to-earth style, Australia's bestselling motivational author, Paul Hanna, shows you how to focus on your dreams and achieve them. You deserve to be successful – here are some of the tools and techniques to attract that success:

- Practise accepting compliments and watch your self-esteem grow
- Learn how to let go of past mistakes and soar above them
- Know that if you expect the best, you'll get it
- Recognise the gift of setbacks and why you need them
- Listen to those wake-up calls – life crises can make you successful
- Discover how to find your true purpose in life

Believe and Achieve! is about getting back to basics and becoming more focused on what you want to achieve in life. It's about not accepting other people's conditioning of you and believing in your goals. More than anything else, *Believe and Achieve!* is about getting that spark back into your life and achieving your dreams.